Making Successful Presentations

PATRICK FORSYTH worked in publishing before moving into marketing training and consultancy. He now runs his own firm Touchstone Training & Consultancy which specializes in work in marketing, sales, and communication skills. He runs a variety of courses helping people to develop presentation skills and works to plan, rehearse, and fine-tune particular presentations with clients. He is the author of a number of successful business books including *How to Negotiate Successfully* (also published by Sheldon Press), *Marketing for Non-Marketing Managers*, *First Things First* – on time management – and *Agreed! – Making management communication persuasive*. He lives and works in London.

Sheldon Business Books

Sheldon Business Books is a list which exists to promote and facilitate the adoption of humane values and equal opportunities integrated with the technical and commercial expertise essential for successful business practice. Both practical and theoretical issues will be explored in jargon-free, soundly reseached books.

The first titles in the series are:
Making Change Work for You
by Alison Hardingham
Taking the Macho Out of Management
by Paddy O'Brien
How to Succeed in Psychometric Tests
by David Cohen
Fit to Work by Paddy O'Brien
How to Avoid Business Failure by Helen Beare
Beyond Total Quality Management
by Larry Reynolds

Patrick Forsyth **Making Successful Presentations**

Sheldon Business Books

sheldon PRESS

First published in Great Britain in 1995 by
Sheldon Press, SPCK, Marylebone Road, London NW1 4DU

© Patrick Forsyth 1995

All rights reserved. No part of this book may be reproduced or transmitted in any form or by any means, electronic or mechanical, including photocopying, recording, or by any information storage and retrieval system, without permission in writing from the publisher.

British Library Cataloguing-in-Publication Data
A catalogue record for this book is available from the British Library
ISBN 0-85969-725-8

Photoset by Deltatype Ltd, Ellesmere Port, Cheshire
Printed in Great Britain at the University Press, Cambridge

Contents

Acknowledgements vii

Introduction 1

one On Your Feet 7

two Calming the Nerves 16

three Be Prepared 28

four Putting it Over 44

five Tricks of the Trade 60

six Making it Visual 89

seven Involvement 101

Afterword 112

Further Information 116

Appendix 117

Index 119

The human brain starts working the moment you are born and never stops until you stand up to speak in public.
Sir George Jessel

For Jacqui:
with thanks for
taking an interest.

Acknowledgements

> It usually takes me three weeks
> to prepare a good impromptu speech
> *Mark Twain*

No one writes a 'how-to' book such as this entirely unaided. Certainly for me, writing about the skill of speaking in public draws on a variety of diverse information and advice received over many years. Looking back I needed every bit of it. If asked early in my career to list the things I felt I would never do, I would unhesitatingly have put making formal presentations at the top of the list. I could not do it, I was convinced I never would and the thought of perhaps ever having to terrified me witless.

Yet for the last twenty or so years, working as a marketing and training consultant, I have spent much of my time 'on my feet', and regularly spent some of it helping to develop presentational skills in others. I am, I suppose, living proof that presentational skills can be learned. Any ability I now have, not only to present myself but to advise on the subject, is a direct result of many different people with whom I have worked over the years, and especially in my early days in consultancy and training. I was fortunate to work in an environment and with people that first thrived on setting and responding to challenges, and second where generosity in the extreme with time and advice made meeting them possible.

Too many people were involved to mention then all individually. But perhaps I could mention David Senton, who recruited me into the consulting world, and who is my Partner now in the firm we formed in 1990. He personifies the inspiration I have drawn from many, and is still an invaluable colleague and a good friend.

So my writing here draws on my own experience of getting to grips with the process of presenting effectively, on the advice I received while so doing and also on the comments and experience of the many clients and course participants with whom I have worked to develop and extend their skills. My thanks therefore to all who played a part in making this possible. In addition, thanks are due to Gower Publishing for permission to adapt, amend, and extend certain elements of my book *Running an Effective Training Session* (Gower, 1992) for inclusion here, and to Constance Lamb, who when not acting runs *Easy Speaking* in London, for clarifying my thought about voice utilization and whom I quote in Chapter Two. And, last but by no means least, I would like to thank my contacts at Sheldon Press. I have worked with them previously and have always found them a pleasure to deal with; Joanna Moriarty in particular provided much appreciated support.

Patrick Forsyth
Touchstone Training & Consultancy
17 Clocktower Mews
Arlington Avenue
London N1 7BB
January 1995

Introduction

> I am the most spontaneous speaker
> in the world because every word, every
> gesture, and every retort has
> been carefully rehearsed
> *George Bernard Shaw*

Making presentations may be fun, or fearsome. Either way they are usually important. Consider them first in the context of business and business success. To achieve success in business an individual has to acquire and deploy a number of necessary skills. Even with that achieved a host of other factors, not least hard work and sometimes a measure of good luck (though this is, of course, more often the reason others are successful), will contribute to the degree of success achieved. Many skills are, of course, job related; a sales person must know how to sell, an accountant must know how to keep the score.

Other skills are common to many occupations, and a few of these have such wide application and are so important that they might be appropriately described as 'career skills'. By this I mean that they play a disproportionate part in whatever mix of circumstances ultimately decides whether individual success will be achieved, or rather to what degree success will occur. Several areas of expertise might be considered to fit this category. A degree of numeracy is now a vital addition to many job specifications. The various skills that are concerned with managing people are vital to some people. And for others there is an increasing need for some degree of computer and keyboard literacy which grows by the day, and is a challenge to many. In addition, several skills that might be considered as career skills are in the area of communications: the ability to write a clear and succinct report, for example. Few would surely argue with the inclusion of one such, and that is the ability to make an effective presentation.

This is a skill which, while widely necessary, still worries many. By no means everyone has an inherent ability to speak on their feet; perhaps the reverse is true. Indeed it is something many find difficult, and some dread. Certainly there can be few worse feelings than rising to your feet to face an audience knowing that you are ill-equipped to do so, unless it is sitting down again all too aware that it has not gone well.

The purpose of presentations

The length of a presentation can vary. It may take a few minutes or be a seminar lasting all day. Similarly, there is a range of possible degrees of formality which may involve speaking to a few key people from the head of the table, or addressing an audience of a hundred or more from the lectern or platform in a conference room. In addition, there are a number of different reasons why a presentation may be necessary. These need not be mutually exclusive, and include the need to:

- inform
- motivate
- instruct
- debate
- persuade
- demonstrate
- build on existing situations and belief

and also more complex objectives such as to change people's attitudes. On occasion *all* these may be involved. Additionally, in business many speakers want the audience to *do* something as a result of hearing what is said. However, there is a danger that simplifying in this way, just saying 'do something', makes the process sound deceptively simple. The truth is there is often a great deal hanging on a presentation.

Presentations can be directed internally or externally. One may be intended to prompt the agreement of the Board to a particular plan of action, another may be intended to persuade a client to place a large order with the organization. Still others to sway a union vote or obtain the support of an outside organization such as a bank. Presentations are important; sometimes very important. And it is not stretching a point to say that plans, careers, financial results, and even the future direction of a whole department or organization can rest on whether a presentation succeeds or not.

So, the ability to make a good presentation, and do so certainly and appropriately to the circumstances, is a key one for very many people. Indeed the trend is for more and more people in organizations to find it a part of their job, from time to time if not regularly. Such people may be from throughout the hierarchy and around the structure of the organization, and these days virtually any job may necessitate the making of occasional or regular presentations as part of its responsibilities. It may not be something that always comes naturally, but it is something that can be learned. Not everyone will succeed in becoming a great orator, but most can acquire the basis to make a workmanlike job of this vital task; and many will surprise themselves with what they can achieve.

For want of a nail

A key characteristic of presentations, and one which makes the point of how necessary it is to be well versed in how to make an effective one, is their inherent fragility. That is to say that the detail of exactly how it is done is important and directly affects the reception it achieves. The success of any presentation can be diluted if a detail is not right. This effect is cumulative; in other words, a number of individual errors can begin to lower the impact a presentation achieves, where one might slip by unnoticed. This dilution can be brought about by an obvious error such as getting the slides in the wrong order or by showing one upside down; or it can stem from a seemingly small matter – as small as the incorrect choice of a single word. As an example, I once heard someone intent on describing and giving a favourable impression of his organization to a group say: 'We offer a *fragmented* range of services . . .'. Whatever he meant (a divisionalized structure arranged to best serve differing customer needs, perhaps) it gave the wrong impression. The word had negative connotations and the group spent a long moment distracted, as they said to themselves: '*Fragmented?*', and paid less attention to the words that followed than the speaker would have wished. This occurrence was made worse because it was virtually the first point made early on in the presentation, and first impressions – as we will see – are disproportionately important.

The effect of such small factors can, of course, also be positive. Just the right turn of phrase, description or flourish can make a point sink home in a way that another delivery would have failed to maximize. Avoiding the first of these and utilizing the second is very much part of the skill that must be acquired by those intent on acquiring sound presentational skills. Presentations, in common with many other areas of expertise, from writing a good report to juggling with flaming torches, demands the learning of those techniques that can help and their successful deployment. Without this there will be disaster, or holes burnt in the carpet. But there is more to it than that.

What makes a good presenter?

What makes someone successful at making presentations? There certainly are tricks of the trade – techniques – just as with many a skill. But it is not a mechanistic thing. It needs confidence (this comes in part from knowing that the techniques are understood). It needs empathy if it is to be pitched in just the right manner for a particular group. It entails interactive aspects, if an audience is to be read and if questions are to be answered. There are certain physical skills involved (even removing and replacing an overhead projector slide has to be done the right way, and done without distracting the presenter from the main task, that of delivering their message). It needs, or must certainly appear to have, clout. In all this there is no substitute for practice. So while the content of the pages that follow will certainly assist, presenting is a practical skill and you will also need opportunities to practise. Indeed, one thought you may find useful is that you should consider seeking out opportunities to make presentations (this especially at the stage when your instincts may say the opposite). This will create opportunities for practice which is ultimately the only way to sustain improvement, and acquire the good habits and reflexes that are the hallmark of the successful presenter.

Most of the training I have conducted during my time as a consultant has had a focus on marketing, sales, and communication skills, and has thus involved me primarily with people from the marketing side of the organizations for which I have worked. But I have also regularly run seminars and workshops to help participants, often from more widely around the organization, to develop effective presentation skills. Such courses have always been among the most satisfying to conduct. Whether those attending are just starting, or whether the workshop involves more experienced people rehearsing a major event, the difference that some guidance makes can often be significant. Because it is such an important skill, it is always rewarding to feel that people leave after some sort of course with greater confidence and skill and the ability to make more effective presentations in future than before their attendance. A wide range of people, exposed to the details of what makes for a professional approach, are able to do better in future almost regardless of the standard they had reached previously. In any case it is not a skill one ever learns completely with no need to further fine-tune performance thereafter. Even those who undertake regular presentations throughout their career go on learning more about it as time goes by (or certainly can do, provided they maintain an open mind).

Because of all this it is usually a well excepted topic amongst potential workshop participants. If you have to make presentations, or if it is clear your job is likely to necessitate this in future, you will want to be able to do it well. This is not simply a desire to see your presentations achieve their objectives, though this doubtless is important. It may well also include a powerful personal desire to be able to undertake the task with less worry. Study of the techniques can help improve performance and thus is valuable in both a personal and job sense, increasing the certainty of a job well done and making the whole process less traumatic. This benefits both the individual and also any organization for which their presentations may be made.

Now, having made the point that presentations are important

and can be difficult, how can you set about making good ones? Chapter One begins to look at the practicalities and also to address some of the most common fears about presenting.

1 On Your Feet

> Talking and eloquence are not the same:
> to speak, and to speak well, are two things
>
> Ben Johnson

All formal presentations involve a group. Matters which you could sit down and run through with one other person, perhaps sitting across the desk, are straightforward by comparison. Actually, that is a simplification. Many meetings and the messages that are communicated in them are not simple to conduct 'off the top of your head', and some of the issues that this book investigates are applicable in the one-to-one situation as well as for presentations. However, let that pass for the moment. It is the group that makes the difference to many people. A sea of faces. Expecting . . . what? Apprehensive? Hostile? Determined to put one over on us? But we are getting ahead of ourselves. We must be clear initially not only about why presentations are so important, but accept that we can influence their outcome and make them work. In fact, as we will see, their importance goes beyond just getting a message across. Even that may not be inherently straightforward. Furthermore, a presentation will say a good deal more than the content of the message; it is the audience that influences every aspect of what must be done to be effective. In this short chapter a number of premises are addressed which are important background to the detail that follows.

The reason for presentations

Consider a typical organization. It can be large or small. It matters little exactly what it does. It could be yours. On a particular day, or during a typical week, some of the items scheduled in the diaries of various executives might include:

- a presentation at a departmental meeting. Perhaps morale is a little low, there are changes to announce, belt-tightening to be instigated or new systems to be explained; the feeling is that the group will resent or be indifferent to what must be done – yet if the reasons for the message are sound it will be important. Changes seen as onerous may in fact act to protect jobs
- a presentation of the annual plan for a section or division is to be made to the Board. Perhaps the hierarchy makes this difficult, perhaps the section feels it is not a major player, perhaps time to make the case and explain the details is limited ('what will they say about the budget?'); despite such feeling the whole of the next operational period will be affected by it and its success, or lack of it – it must go well
- a presentation is to be made to a major customer. A significant percentage of the annual turnover is dependent on this customer's loyalty, yet the market is increasingly competitive, product and service are being subjected to a harsh appraisal; the customer's judgement will inevitably be affected by the quality of the presentation – a good one will be interpreted as indicative of good service to come, a poor one might put the whole relationship in question, and there are eager competitors waiting on the sidelines
- a short briefing session is scheduled to explain details of the organization's move to new offices. The move is being made for all the right reasons, yet inevitably poses short-term problems of organizing for and coping with the move itself, and also raises personal fears in some as to 'what the new place will be like and where will I sit?'; if people co-operate enthusiastically it will all go more smoothly – they need to accept the move and see the advantages.

These four are typical of the sort of thing that takes place in organizations everywhere day in, day out. Such a list might include a dozen more situations: a press briefing, a training session, meetings giving advance notice of changes, canvassing support or issuing instructions. It could also include social matters: a retirement party or welcome to a new employee, all demanding an appropriate presentation to be made.

In all these cases the importance of the presentation and its quality is very clear. And it is not simply a corporate importance, it is a personal one too for whoever is on their feet. Reputations will be enhanced or diluted in the process, the effect is on the outward aspect of corporate profile – and because of this presentation skill is what was referred to in the Introduction as a 'career' skill. But there are also more personal implications. For the inexperienced, uninformed or untried speaker the process is inclined to be not just difficult. It can be literally frightening; and the fact that some of the fears are – if analysed – irrational helps but little to dispel them. We know, if we think about it, that the ground is not going to open up under our feet so that we sink without trace – though there may be other moments when we pray that it will!

Making it go well

So, two things can be taken as given. First, that presentations are important. This may seem something that it is impossible to ignore (it is not: more of this later) and is certainly amongst the reasons that making presentation can be a traumatic process. If you are in any way wary of them be assured that you are completely normal. Most speakers, even the most experienced, have fears to some degree. With experience comes the ability to deal with those fears, and minimize if not totally remove them.

Second, presentations must go well. Let me rephrase that for it must be seen in a specific way: *you* must *make* them go well. Short of delegation – which will never always be possible even for the most senior – there is no other way.

Further, there may be comparatively few 'born speakers', but there are an increasing number of people who have come to make a pretty good job of it and many who are more than workmanlike. As I said in the Acknowledgements, I am living proof that presentational ability can be acquired, even by the most reluctant person. Those speakers you perhaps regard as naturals almost certainly have one thing in common; they work at it. The techniques involved (many as we will see both common sense and simple) really do help. They help both to smooth and polish the presentation itself and to make it psychologically easier to deal with. An understanding of the process, and of the details of what makes it go well, what achieves particular effects and how to both work at the detail and orchestrate the whole, is the foundation for good performance. Of course, practice helps too, and practice provides more experience more quickly if you understand what is going on, and why what you are doing is working or not quite hitting the mark. The following, a roughly verbatim recollection of the introduction to a short talk I once gave, highlights and contrasts the skills and the lack of them.

> Business is all very well but it has a habit of involving us in things that we do not really like. Not just distasteful things like reducing two filing cabinets full of paper to one drawer's worth without throwing away anything vital, or filling in the VAT returns, but others we feel ill equipped to do well. In communications, many are confident of talking about their business in many circumstances, but in a formal presentation situation they may go to pieces.
>
> They stumble, they hesitate, they sweat. They begin every sentence with the word 'Basically'. They say 'Um, er . . . at this moment in time we are making some progress with the necessary preliminary work prior to the establishment of the initial first phase of work' when they mean: 'We plan to start soon'. Just when they should be blinding the audience with their expertise, they upset or confuse them. If the presentation is to customers (or prospects), or any important group, it really matters. At worst people go on too long, get faster and faster towards the end in a desperate attempt to finish on the day they started. Or their explanations leave people bemused, they pick holes in someone in the group (or worse, their nose). Their slides cannot be read from the back of the room without a telescope, and the only long word of which they appear ignorant is 'rehearsal'.
>
> Of course to others, making a potent, persuasive and powerful presentation is second nature. They know their stuff and the rules of how to put it over. The first rule is always to assume the audience is as thick as they look, and will, provided

they hit the right level of seemingly clever but impenetrable jargon, instantly conclude they are in the presence of an expert. Of course, they recognize that some care is necessary if people are to get the gist of their argument. So they talk v-e-r-y s-l-o-w-l-y to make a point, use simple words and generally treat the group as if they had the brains of dormice. They spell out complicated bits by talking painfully IN CAPITAL LETTERS. Though they are always careful not to be condescending about this and upset people – you *do* know what condescending means, don't you?

For these 'natural' presenters being on their feet is something to savour. They need only the briefest of introductions and they are away, moving quickly past the first slide ('Sorry that's the wrong way up, but you can see what it says I am sure'), the loose change in their pockets rattling at ninety decibels and not a note in sight. Makes others feel in awe and sadly inadequate – even the famous: it was Mark Twain who said: 'It usually takes me three weeks to prepare a good impromptu speech'. Poor chap; just as well he was better at writing.

Such speakers should not hog the limelight just because it is fun. If you are in this category give your colleagues a chance. Next time someone says 'We need a presentation' pick on and give the job to whoever displays the least enthusiasm. It will do them good, and besides there is nothing like inflicting sheer terror on a colleague to make you feel superior. So don't bother to give them any notice, that would spoil the fun. Just put them in front of a suitable group, for example some demanding prospects who would rather give their business to a troop of performing chimps than to anyone who apparently cannot explain the simplest point clearly. Without their understanding how to go about it, this will be like pushing them into the lions' den; before feeding time. They will quickly find themselves in deep trouble. No audience will warm to a speaker who is ill prepared, and flounders through a talk that is poorly constructed and badly delivered. Next time it will be someone else's turn to discover that once in the lions' den, getting out of it cannot be guaranteed by simply saying: 'Nice pussycat' . . .

Formal presentation may not seem to be something that comes naturally to you, but it is something you *will* be able to do. What is set out in this book aims specifically to make it easier, more certain and even more fun.

The first step to improving whatever presentational ability you may currently have is perhaps to see it as something you *can* change. No one is born with a ready made instant appreciation of what makes for good presentation (well, very few and if you were one of those you would be unlikely to be reading this). Like so much else that is worthwhile doing some effort is required to put yourself in a position to achieve a particular standard or to do better – and this is an on-going factor with a skill that can really always be improved, there being no such thing as the perfect presentation. On the other hand, working at it need not be too onerous or time-consuming and the results, as we have already seen, make some effort very worthwhile. Before moving on to the principles that make the whole process work, two other factors are worth holding in mind.

Perception *is* reality

Somewhere there is an old saying: 'what you see is what you get'. This certainly has relevance here with regard to presentations. Consider by way of example someone selling a service: an accountant, designer or architect perhaps. In such fields it is common for people to have to make competitive presentations as potential clients ascertain which of a short-list of potential suppliers they will use.

If such a presentation is inexpertly done, the prospect does not think to themselves 'what an excellent designer, what a shame they cannot make a better presentation'; rather they say: 'what a rotten presentation, I bet their design work isn't very good'. In other words other abilities – and a wide range of them – are judged from people's ability to present. This may not be fair, or even reasonable; but it is what happens. There is no response but to maximize the impact of presentations carried out to avoid this effect. It does not only occur in overtly sales situations (and in the example it is particularly important because a service by its nature cannot be tested, so the impact of the people involved is crucial), it occurs every time someone gets to their feet to address a group. The audience immediately begins to draw conclusions and make judgements about the person, their general competence and specific abilities. The perceptions that a person engenders are powerfully moulded if they have to present, much more so than in general business toing and froing.

The plus side of this, of course, is that good presentational standards enhance the perception of ability in other areas. By using the appropriate techniques, by putting on a professional show, you can positively and actively build your image generally and increase the chances of acceptance for anything which you are promoting. This is true externally or internally to the organization and of any group one can think of as an audience. It is a fact that no presenter can afford to forget.

Communication and the audience

Communication, whether one-to-one or with a group, is not easy, or rather the difficulty is to make communication clear and understandable (see what I mean). It is a very easy difficulty to underestimate. Everybody tends to think that they can communicate (rather as you never meet anyone – or certainly no man – who will admit to being a bad driver). After all we all do it all the time, especially in organizations. But in fact, without care, communication can so easily deteriorate into confusion and misunderstanding. There must be hundreds of examples of communication failure despite the best intentions of the communicator:

- there is the note left for the milkman saying: 'Please deliver an extra pint today. If this note blows away, please ring bell.'
- there is the story of the journalist, researching a feature on Hollywood, sending a brief telex: 'HOW OLD CARY GRANT?'; in due course the message comes back: 'OLD CARY GRANT FINE; HOW ARE YOU?'
- there is also the wonderful phrase, usually attributed to the late ex-US President Nixon: 'I know that you understand what you think I said, but I am not sure that you realize that what you heard is not what I meant.'

You can doubtless think of many more. Such stories make a point. Communication is never easy, and on your feet it can be just that bit more difficult as your tongue seems to run away on its own as nerves overpower precision, and what started as a careful explanation comes out as garbled and convoluted. Many a speaker has sat down disappointed with the presentation they have just made and *knowing* they could have explained something so much better, one-to-one, or in writing or just with a little longer to get it right. If you have done even a little presenting you do not need to be told that it is different on your feet; you know that this is true.

All this has a bearing on the audience. They *want* to understand and become restless as well as confused if they do not. The audience is vital to any presenter and we will return to them in later pages; here suffice it to say that there are a number of immediate factors to be borne in mind:

- *hearing* is not perfect, not in the medical sense, but because people's concentration wanders. It is just not possible to concentrate continuously (when did your attention last flit away from reading this?), but a speaker who recognizes this and intentionally sets out to retain the group's interest will do better than one who ignores the fact
- even when people hear they *dilute* the message as it is filtered through their existing expectations, knowledge, experience, and prejudices; thus new or unfamiliar ideas will need more careful presentation than those which are already well accepted
- *conclusions* may be drawn before the full case has been put across (and the *status quo* is always difficult to overturn).

That said the presenter can potentially get over these factors. Again much that is to follow here is relevant, but at this stage a few points are worth noting, the presenter must:

- look the part: that means having an appearance which the audience associates with authority, expertise or whatever it is that is trying to be projected, rather than what the speaker regards as comfortable or fashionable (I would not presume to say much more about how you should look, but would

suggest you consider objectively what a powerful part of your assessment of others this is and act appropriately)
- come over as a good presenter – because, as has been said, poor presentation skills have other weaknesses read from them
- actually be clear and interesting (or any other adjective the audience would wish to deploy)

and have respect for the audience in everything from a seeming ability to stick to time, to a concentration on what they will find interesting and the most appropriate way to put it across – to any particular group.

The audience, we will find, must be kept perpetually in mind as all the various aspects of presentation are contemplated. Not only that, but a presentation that is genuinely audience oriented will always go down better that something introspective, and may well prove easier to prepare and give as well.

In fact, having harped on some of the difficulties, there is perhaps one thing worse to contemplate than being on your feet as the Chairperson says 'And now, over to . . .' feeling hopelessly ill-equipped to undertake the presentation that must follow. And that is to be in the audience when such a presentation takes place. Really, think about it; it is not just tedious or boring, it is embarrassing, sometimes in the extreme. Think about what that means: the audience, the group, whoever they are, *want you to succeed*. It is easy to consider the audience the opposition, but, with a few exceptions perhaps (for example, political situations in an organization), they are not. They are the reason for the presentation, they want it to go well and you can use this fact to help make it do just that.

This fact is always worth keeping in mind. In the next chapter we turn to the question of the speaker's 'nerves', and not regarding the audience as the opposition is perhaps the first step to overcoming these nerves.

2 Calming the Nerves

If they liked you, they didn't applaud
– they just let you live
Bob Hope

Speaking in public is, as has been said, inclined to be regarded as traumatic. Indeed it can engender a particularly emotional response in many, and serious (or semi-serious) surveys regularly show it to rank high in terms of overall fears, following closely on death and divorce. Few speakers, and this includes the most experienced, would claim to be able to make a presentation with *no* nerves. Some will say a lack of nerves is not only unlikely, it is undesirable; they need the adrenalin to carry them along.

Others have vivid visions of their worst fears:

> The previous speaker is near to concluding. You cannot seem to concentrate on what he is saying. You run over your opening remarks in your mind for the twenty-seventh time, and, thus distracted, you suddenly hear the Chairman calling your name. You leap to your feet sending your notes scattering to the winds. Panic-stricken, you grovel on the floor and collect them up, half trip up the steps to the platform and take your place behind the lectern. Your rescued pages seem to sit precariously on the slim lip of the sloping rack, and your hands are shaking so much that you dare not try to straighten them.
>
> You make a start: 'Good morning, Gadies and Lentlemen'. Your mouth is dry and you do not seem to be able to catch your breath. You put up your first slide and it is immediately apparent that those in the rear half of the room cannot read it – though everyone notices it is upside down. Having corrected that you are pretty sure they all notice that the word 'Agenda' is spelt with a J.

At this point things start to go wrong.

You notice that the clock at the back of the room stopped hours ago and can offer you no guidance, you lose your place in your notes, and turn over to the next page only to find it has got out of order. At which point the papers fall to the floor . . . seemingly in slow motion, and your voice dries completely; the butterflies struggle from your stomach and begin to fly around the room. As one dive-bombs the Chairman he sounds an air raid siren and . . .

Wake up. It is not really happening. Indeed hopefully no one has ever experienced all of this in the same ten minutes. Though mistakes do occur – I remember once driving all the way to Birmingham, a terrible journey in the pouring rain, arriving at the venue I was to speak at only just in time, hastening in and opening my file to check my carefully prepared notes. Carefully prepared they might have been – but they were not for the talk I was scheduled to give that day! Well nobody is perfect.

So, how do you avoid all this?

Making it easier

First, be assured that it is avoidable. All, or certainly the vast majority, of these problems can be avoided. Because, although I have (I hope) exaggerated in the passage above, everyone commonly has some fears and it is appropriate to deal with this aspect of making a presentation now ahead of getting down to the positive ways you can make everything go well. After all, in real life it is difficult to concentrate on a considered approach if you have real reservations about what lies ahead, much less if you are shaking like a leaf. Having said that I am going to cheat and leave one of the cures to a later stage. What is that? in a word: preparation.

It is worth emphasizing. Preparation is the surest way to ensure all goes well and minimize nerves. The key reason for nerves is the fear that something will go wrong. Prepare well and quite simply you then *know* that a whole range of elements *will* go well. Consider an example from my nightmare above. You will never be put out by discovering that a slide cannot be read from the back of the room if you try it out beforehand. You are less likely to muddle your notes if you number the pages, less likely still if you fasten the pages together or put them securely in some sort of file or binder.

So, we return to the detail of how to undertake your preparation in the next chapter. Before leaving it therefore and dealing with other matters, let me link it to another vital factor: that of confidence. Now confidence is a useful foundation to everything you have to do in speaking formally, and preparation – the security of knowing it is done well, thoroughly and will help – breeds confidence. This becomes a virtuous circle. Sound preparation creates confidence, more confidence makes for a better start, a good start boosts your confidence to continue . . . and so on.

It is not just nerves . . .

Regularly in my work in conducting courses to help people develop their presentation skills, I ask participants what factors they feel make them uneasy about presenting. Be reassured *everyone* has some fears. The commonest stated usually include:

- butterflies in the stomach
- a dry mouth making it difficult to speak
- not knowing where to put your hands
- fear of the reaction of the audience
- fear of not having enough material
- fear of not being able to get through the material in the time
- not knowing how loud to pitch your voice
- losing your place
- over-, or under-, running on time
- being asked questions you cannot answer
- drying up.

All these main ones that seem to concern people are worth a specific comment (in some cases referring on to more detailed comment to come). Whether such things are real fears for you or just cause minor concern, the view to take of all this is a practical one. There are actions that actually sort and remove some of these problems, others are helped by the way you organize the speaking environment, something which is explained later in this chapter, and also has a considerable effect on your ability to overcome any nerves.

What about the ones my course participants mention quoted above?

- *Butterflies in the stomach*: this is a physical manifestation of any worries you may have. In mild form it does no harm and fades as the adrenalin starts to flow when you get underway. On the other hand a number of practical measures undoubtably help reduce the feeling. Some are seemingly small, perhaps obvious; they do work, however, and may work better when some are used together. They include:

- a few deep breaths just before you start
- no heavy food too soon before you start
- no starvation diets, or the butterflies will be accompanied by rumbles
- no alcohol (some would say very little) before the off

and the confidence of knowing you are well prepared and organized.

- *Dry mouth*: again this is a natural reaction, but one simply cured. Just take a sip of water before you start. And never be afraid of asking for, or organizing, a supply of water in front of you. Place it where you are least likely to spill it and you may, like me, prefer to avoid the fashionably fizzy waters supplied by many of the venues where speakers often find themselves, especially hotels and conference centres. I am sure it is nice for the audience and offered with good intentions, but it is inclined to make you burp if you are the speaker. The longer the duration of your talk, the more you will need to take the occasional sip. Talking makes you dry and an air-conditioned venue or office compounds the problem. Act accordingly.

- *Somewhere to put your hands*: somehow they can feel awkward. They seem like disproportionately large lumps at the end of your arms. The trick here is to avoid obvious awkwardness, give yourself something to do with them and then *forget* about

More and more

Initially most people have a clearly graduated reaction to numbers in the audience. A few are not *so* bad, you can equate them to a round table meeting, more begins to seem more difficult, and a large number is 'a terrifying sea of faces'. Why so? After all the job of the speaker is very similar regardless of the numbers present. Not only may you have a similar message to get over, but to a large extent you need to do it in a similar way.

The best rule for talking to a large group is *to treat it like a smaller one*. For example:

- eye contact is important, and with a larger group the scale of applying it is larger too, but the principle is identical
- be yourself. This is important for any presentation. You may want to exaggerate a little, and an expansive gesture may need to be that little more expansive in a packed conference room, but do not change your basic style because of the numbers. It is easier for you to be natural and the impression given is better for the audience; all of them.
- use feedback. If there are more people there will be more of it, somewhere in the audience there will be an enthusiastic response to focus on
- use involvement. Of course, the appropriate level of formality varies, but there is no real reason not to say: 'What do you think about this?' and prompt a comment or three from an audience of a hundred than there is from one of a dozen. Or not to focus on individuals if that is appropriate: 'John Black is here somewhere – where are you John? and what do you think?'; especially if they will appreciate it
- do not let sheer numbers put you off anything that the presentation needs, for example if you need to pause . . . pause, do not let the pressure of many eyes make you spoil what may be an important emphasis
- think of the total audience in sub-sections, use eye contact to focus on small groups within the audience, then pretend to yourself that you are talking to just the six at the back or the three in the front row.

Of course, you need to doublecheck certain things carefully with a large group (e.g. the microphone or the acoustics), otherwise relax and do not let it worry you. It is, in any case, the kind of thing that is more of a worry before you do it than while you are doing it. If you present appropriately to the subject, the occasion and the audience, then the number present need not change things greatly. Everyone in any group is an individual. Talk to them as individuals and there is no reason why they should not all be satisfied.

them. A man should remember that while one hand in a pocket may look all right, both hands in pockets always appears slovenly. More about hands in Chapter Five.

- *Audience reaction*: or rather the fear of a negative one. Ask yourself *why* they should react negatively. The fear may be irrational. It may be because you feel ill prepared – we have touched on preparation. And anyway remember that audiences hate poor presentations; they *want* you to succeed (see box opposite).

- *Not having enough material*: this should simply not be a fear. Your preparation will mean you *know* you have not only enough but the right amount of material for the topic and the time.

- *Having too much material*: this needs no separate comment from the previous point, except to say that even if you start with too much, preparation should whittle it down to the appropriate amount.

- *Not knowing how loud to speak*: this may be a reasonable fear in a strange room, but you can test it – ahead of the meeting find someone to stand at the back and check how you come over until you get the level right. In fact, a moment's thought shows that it is not a very difficult problem. If the only person in the room was at the far end you would probably speak to them naturally at just the right level. Try not to worry and think of yourself as addressing the back row (though remember to switch off, I sometimes go home after a day conducting a course and am told 'Don't shout, you are not talking to the back row now').

- *Losing your place*: again there are practical measures to help, apart from knowing your message well, particularly in terms of the exact format of speaker's notes you have in front of you (this is of major importance: see Chapter Three).

- *Misjudging the timing*: in part an accurate judgement of time comes with practice. If you find it difficult do not despair, you will get better and better at it. Remember timing is important, and particularly not overrunning – a common fault – is a virtue that is appreciated by many – even in the most entertaining speech; and is vital at, say, a conference when the whole day's events can be put out by one undisciplined speaker.

- *Being asked questions you cannot answer*: no one is expected to be omniscient. Dealing with questions is dealt with in Chapter Seven. Here let me make the one point that it is not the end of the world to say: 'I don't know' – always an important point for any would-be presenter to accept.

- *Drying up*: here one must address the reason for it. Dry mouth? Pause and have a sip of water, no one will mind. Lost your place? If that does not happen you will not dry up. Just nerves? Well, some of the elements now mentioned – and preparation – will help. It is worth remembering here that time often seems to flow at a different rate for presenters and audiences. Often during presentations courses, where usually I am using video to record and allow discussion about what participants do, people will regularly criticize themselves about one perceived fault: 'I dried up at one stage' they say, 'there was an awful great gap'. Yet no one noticed except them, and often when the video is replayed they cannot even spot where it happened. It just seemed too long.

In terms of attitude you should note that you need a practical approach to all these sorts of feelings. Just feeling 'I'm worried' is difficult to combat. Ask yourself why you are worried and you may well surprise yourself, discovering that there is a practical solution that will remove or reduce whatever factor is creating the feeling. With that principle in mind we turn to another area in which the right action can reduce worries and act to create a comfortable climate in which you can present more easily.

Organizing the environment

By this I mean not the Green issues, but the speaking environment, the room and particularly the immediate area you inhabit at the front of the room. If you work to ensure you are comfortable with all the arrangements that affect you, there is at once much less to distract your mind; all of which can then focus on the job in hand. If not . . . well imagine some of the hazards of this sort:

> The table in front of you is narrow. It has an overhead projector standing firmly in its centre, and there is little room for your notes and slides. There is no time to reorganize the layout, so you perch your papers on a corner, and begin to place used overhead projector slides on a chair a little to one side. You are well prepared in most ways but your mind constantly flits from one hazard to the next: are your papers safe? are you reaching far enough to put things safely on the chair? have you remembered exactly where the curling wire from the projector to the power main lies? why is the water jug perched on a saucer two sizes too small and why, like so many jugs, will it not pour without cascading ice cubes far and wide?
>
> At the same time you attempt to keep small portions of your mind on the time, maintain eye contact with members of the group and . . . your foot catches – just slightly – the electric cable, enough to move the projector an inch or two to one side and knock the water jug . . .

But your own imagination can no doubt do better (or worse?). None of this should happen. It needs thought and planning and the precise arrangement will depend on the circumstances and such things as whether there is a lectern, but you can and should create an arrangement as near to your ideal as the situation allows. Two categories of thinking and action are necessary or desirable here:

- *Prior selection and arrangement of key physical factors*:
  - whether you want to use a lectern or not
  - equipment in the right place (overhead projector (OHP) or viewgraph, flipchart or anything else that may be involved)
  - equipment tested and working
  - hazards removed or taped down (e.g. electric wires)
  - water in a safe place
  - sufficient space for all you want to do (notes, slides etc.)

- acoustics checked (finding out how loud to speak has been mentioned).

The above are basic; more may occur to you and others may be necessary in special circumstances. For instance, is there a clock you can see? (If not you may want to take off your wristwatch and lay it in front of you to avoid looking visibly – pointedly – at it on your wrist.) Can you easily see any necessary signals from the Chair? Can you signal to anyone necessary (a secretary at the back who will summon the refreshments)? It may be worth your making a short checklist of the things that are important to the kind of presentation you have to make, and the location(s) in which you usually find yourself conducting them.

Note: certain things need organizing differently depending on whether one is left- or right-handed. To work an OHP neatly, being right-handed, I need to stand to the left of it (as I face it). This is one factor to watch out for, especially if you are at an outside venue – in twenty or more years of working regularly in hotels to accommodate courses I have never been asked by the hotel staff whether I am right- or left-handed and often equipment is set up inappropriately.

- *What suits you*: by this I mean not just things which you personally find create comfort for you (it does not matter if others are left cold by them) but that you just *like* – what you might think of as personal comfort factors. For example, I find I speak regularly from behind a standard height table. Fine, one of reasonable width usually gives plenty of room for notes, slides, projector and more. But if I lay any notes I have flat on the table then I cannot see them clearly if they are in standard typewriter-sized type. I wear spectacles and have found that if I lay my briefcase on the table and put notes on that, just four or five inches higher, then I can focus at a glance. It suits me, looks fine and is easy to arrange.

    Such 'likes' can become something of a personal fetish. You *must* have certain things just right to be a hundred per cent comfortable. Clearly if this feeling gets too strong it becomes a problem, you do not always have control of everything and sometimes conditions are not ideal. You do not want this to throw you. On the other hand, I think perhaps that if you are inclined to nerves it is actually useful to invent a few such things; organizing them your way gives a small but useful feeling of satisfaction and you can start off feeling you are, in a sense, on familiar ground.

As a final point here note that going into an unfamiliar room just before you speak is to be avoided. What you have perhaps assumed is that it will be a well-equipped meeting room, yet it turns out to be the very opposite and you find yourself in less than ideal circumstances and with no time to correct them. If it is your meeting there is less problem (and no excuse for not checking); if you are a guest never be afraid to raise issues with the Chair or organizer. They are normally only too happy to make some small changes if they will make you more comfortable.

Your voice

Another source of concern to some is their voice, or rather the projection of it. Public speaking should not be a strain. If it is then it will show, the audience will hear the strain and may even read it wrongly, believing you to be uncertain perhaps just when you want to sound authoritative.

Again, this should not be a problem. You may feel your voice is inadequate to the task, but it almost certainly will do the job supremely well. As an actor I know once said to me: listen to children in the playground. They all have huge voices, seemingly endless lung capacity and projecting their voice causes them no problem at all. Why should that change with age? If it does then it is because the wrong habits build up. The solution is relaxation and breathing.

Here I will plunder my actor friend's views again. Constance Lamb not only acts but runs public speaking sessions for a variety of individuals and groups, many in business, to improve their presentations skill. I asked her what the key factors here are; she told me:

Most people do not breathe properly when they speak. The breath supports the voice and has plenty of power and energy. If you speak on the 'held' breath, this creates tension and stress in the voice and blocks off the power. You will create the best impact by speaking on the outward breath by using the diaphragm – the muscle that can best be described as the 'kicker', and which propels the breath and the voice outwards. Only in this way can an actor use their voice to fill a large theatre, and it also helps control nerves. If the technique will cope with that then no presenter should have a great problem.

It is easy to demonstrate this to yourself. If you receive a shock, you automatically breathe in sharply by contracting the diaphragm, then 'hold' the breath without letting go. Try it. Take a sharp breath. Hold it. You will find that some tension soon starts to creep in. Now breathe out with a big, audible sigh. The diaphragm relaxes and the tension vanishes. Often everyday speech happens on the held breath, and the breath is only released after we complete a sentence.

The best way to project is to speak during the exhalation of a breath. Try it. Notice the difference. Proper breathing – in slowly through the mouth, expanding the rib cage front, back and sides – imagine the rib cage is like a bellows – is the only way to obtain sufficient air when speaking. It fills the lungs fully and easily. And fast. Taking a few slow, deep breaths like this before you start a talk, particularly if you consciously relax the shoulders and chest as you do so, will relax you.

With this working well you can concentrate on using your voice to produce the modulation and the emphasis any formal presentation needs. Certain potential problems can be cured simply by the manner in which you speak. For example, a person who habitually speaks too fast has only to articulate words (and especially consonants) and pronounce the endings of words clearly, and the pace slows automatically.

All good advice, and some of these points are picked up again in Chapter Five. The voice is the vehicle for your messages and to attempt to make presentations with no conscious thought of it is akin to setting out on a car journey without checking the petrol gauge.

Finally, let me link again all that has been said in this chapter back to preparation. Perhaps the greatest antidote to nerves is to know you are thoroughly and well prepared. If you know what you are going to talk about (and what you will omit), how you are going to go through the message – in detail, the order, where you will exemplify or illustrate etc. – and have related this to the audience to whom you will speak, the timing and other circumstances and have some suitable notes in front of you – then instead of rising to your feet thinking 'I hope this will be all right' you can do so thinking 'I believe this is going to go well'. Having done your homework (as it were) your confidence will rise and outweigh your uncertainties. You will never get rid of every last butterfly, but you should not have your mind distracted by groundless fears and matters that can be organized away, when you need all your concentration on the main task in hand, that of putting your ideas across effectively.

You may (presently) be unaccustomed to public speaking; but you should never be unprepared.

3 Be Prepared

> It usually takes me three weeks
> to prepare a good impromptu speech
> *Mark Twain*

Preparation is a grand word for engaging the brain before the mouth. But it is vital. It makes all the difference between a professional presentation and an indifferent one; or, at worst, an awkward and embarrassing experience. It does not just have to be done, it has to be done thoroughly. It has to be done right. Few, if any, business skills come down to the application of any one 'magic formula'. Would that life were so simple! With presentations however, preparation must come close – it is crucial and should never be skimped.

No one wants what appears to be a well considered dramatic pause to be a wild groping for what on earth should come next. And it is difficult to concentrate on anything – still less inject some sort of flourish – when some failure of preparation is distracting you from something basic such as what comes next. In this chapter we review some of the key tasks of preparation and the way of going about them. In dissecting the process there is a danger that it appears complex or at least lengthy. The reverse is actually true. A systematic approach makes preparation simpler, and once you build up certain habits you will find that your preparation becomes a more and more manageable time in relation to the duration of the presentation you have to make. First things first – the first task seems simple, but a systematic approach is even helpful in terms of assembling the message.

One point needs to be made firmly at this stage. Preparation does not mean starting at the beginning and writing out what you intend to say from beginning to end verbatim. Even if this was done it might lead to the speaker being tempted to read the text, and this is not likely to make for a good overall effect. There are exceptions to this (when the need for precision demands what is said must have word for word accuracy) but these are not the norm. Besides reading something aloud with clarity is, in fact, very difficult for most, as it tends to sound stilted and stifle any animation that should be present.

So it should be made a rule: *do not write out the presentation in full and do not read it.* That said, how do you prepare? A systematic approach is suggested, one that might best be described as moving from the general to the particular, or from outline and key skeleton points to fully fleshed talk. And the starting point is to have a clear objective.

Setting objectives

Regularly when I run sessions to help improve presentations skills, I find I have participants in the session who, whatever their other strengths or weaknesses, fail to deliver the standard of presentation they want because – and sometimes *solely* because – they do not have clear objectives. Objectives are not what you wish to say, they are what you wish to *achieve*.

For example, a manager may need to address a staff meeting of some sort about a new policy. The task is almost certainly not simply to tell them about the policy, more likely it is to ensure they understand the change and how it works, accept the necessity for it and are promptly able to undertake future work in a way that fits the new policy.

The latter view is surely more likely to make preparing a presentation easier and surer. Simplistically we might immediately see such a talk making five points:

- some background to the change
- an explanation of why it is necessary (perhaps in terms of the good things it will achieve)
- exactly what it is and how it works
- the effect on the individual
- what action needs to be taken.

If you think of something like a new procedure for handling customer complaints, or any sensitive or complicated issue, then the danger of some detail being omitted or inadequately dealt with (or understood) is at once clear. Given a more precise case, objectives should always be, as a much quoted acronym has it, SMART. That is:

Specific

Measurable

Achievable

Realistic and

Timed.

And they should have a clear focus on the audience: it is more important to think about what will work for them, rather than what it is *you* want in isolation. Thus you might regard objectives in this light for your reading of this book as:

- to enable you to ensure your future presentations come over in a way that will be seen by their audiences as appropriate and informative (*specific*)
- to ensure (*measurable*) action occurs afterwards (e.g. certain future presentations might be measured by the number of customers placing an order or the number of people agreeing to attend a further meeting after they have heard them)
- that it is right for you, providing sufficient information and ideas in a manageable form for you to really be able to make a difference to what you do in future (providing an *achievable* objective)
- to be not just achievable – possible – but *realistic*, that is, desirable (e.g. here the time it takes to read the book, thus taking you away from other matters, might be compared with the possible gains from so doing – if it took, say, a couple of days this might well be over-engineering)
- and *timed*: when are you going to review (in part by reading the book) how you go about presentations? After all, results cannot come from such a review until it has occurred.

Potential presenters must always be able to answer questions such as:

- why am I doing this? (so that people are better informed)
- what am I trying to achieve? (put them in a position to take, willingly and effectively, a particular action)

about what they plan to present. If you do this and if you find the answer is too unspecific, then the internal conversation needs extending, saying: *which means that* after your first answer and continuing with more explicit descriptions until a real description (away from the simple: 'this is a talk about elephants') is found that truly answers the question.

Once that is clear, then the real task of deciding what is to be said can begin and must, as has been said earlier, be carried through systematically, creating a skeleton and then adding the 'flesh' to produce the complete message. See figure 1 which illustrates this graphically.

Deciding what to say

A four-stage approach does the job of composition well, and is likely to make preparation quicker and more certain.

(i) Listing

This consists of ignoring any thoughts about sequence or structure and simply listing everything – every point – which it might be desirable or necessary to say (perhaps bearing something about the duration and level of detail involved in mind). This, a process that is sometimes referred to as 'mindmapping', gets all the elements involved down on paper. It may need more than one session to complete it. A gap sometimes stimulates the thinking, and certainly you will find one thought leading to another. This could be simply a list, a column of points going down the page. Or you may find it works better in accommodating the developing picture to adopt a 'freestyle' approach, as shown in figure 2. When this is done you can proceed to the next stage.

i) First list the main points

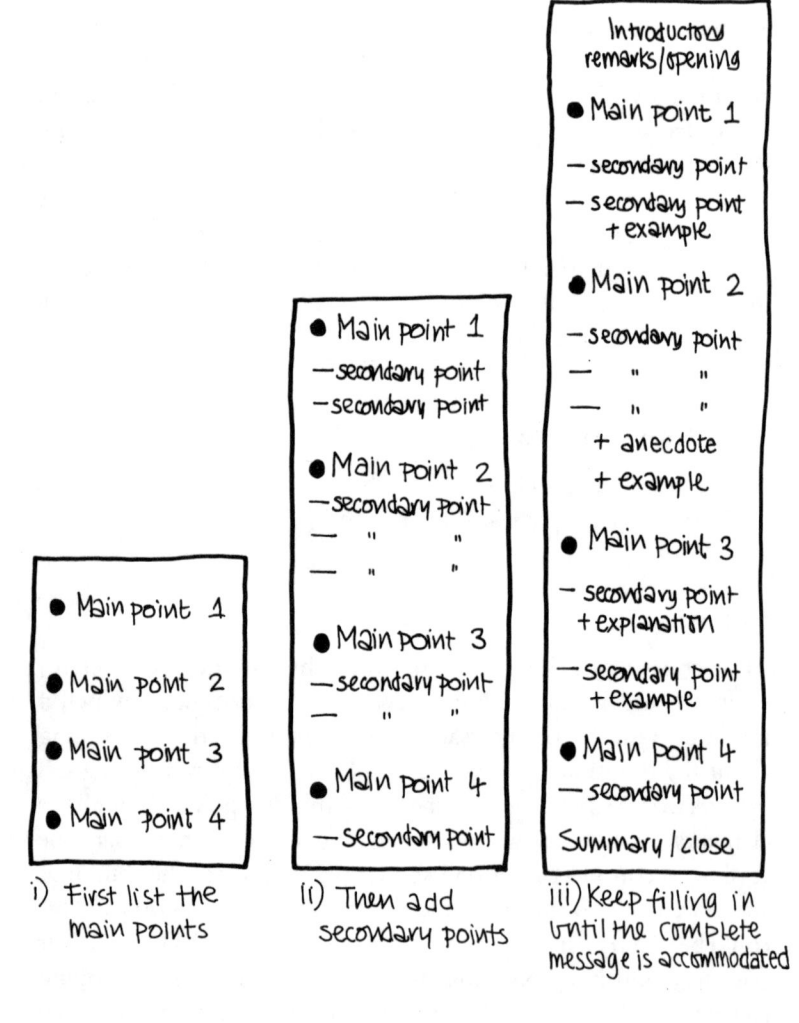

- Main point 1
- Main point 2
- Main point 3
- Main point 4

ii) Then add secondary points

- Main point 1
  - secondary point
  - secondary point
- Main point 2
  - secondary point
  - " "
  - " "
- Main point 3
  - secondary point
  - " "
- Main point 4
  - secondary point

iii) Keep filling in until the complete message is accommodated

Introductory remarks/opening

- Main point 1
  - secondary point
  - secondary point + example
- Main point 2
  - secondary point
  - " "
  - " "
  - + anecdote
  - + example
- Main point 3
  - secondary point + explanation
  - secondary point + example
- Main point 4
  - secondary point

Summary/close

Figure 1. *Putting 'flesh' on the structure*

Figure 2. *Listing: example of 'freestyle' approach to this stage of preparation*

Rather than write a list (which tends to prompt you to think sequentially) the best starting point is to note all the possible topics/points 'freestyle' around the page. The example here imagines the first part of a short presentation about sales effectiveness to illustrate the idea:

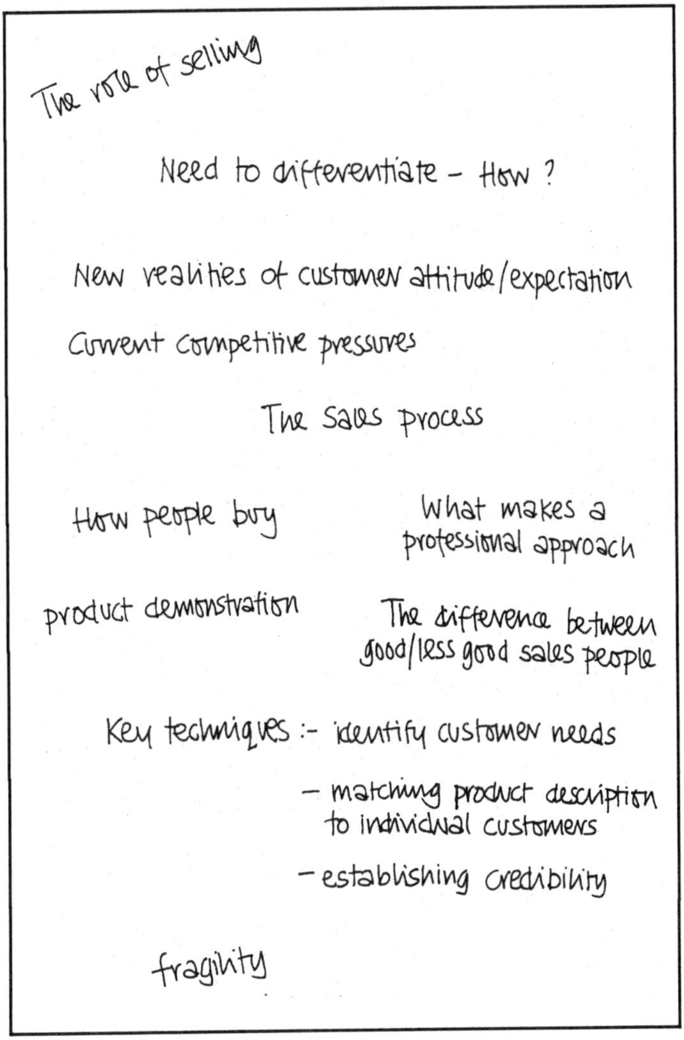

```
The role of selling

            Need to differentiate - How?

      New realities of customer attitude/expectation

      Current competitive pressures

                The sales process

  How people buy          What makes a
                          professional approach

  product demonstration   The difference between
                          good/less good sales people

      Key techniques :- identify customer needs

                       - matching product description
                         to individual customers

                       - establishing credibility

        fragility
```

Figure 3. *Sorting: example of this stage of preparation*

The example of the previous boxed paragraph is continued, showing the annotation that might be added at this stage:

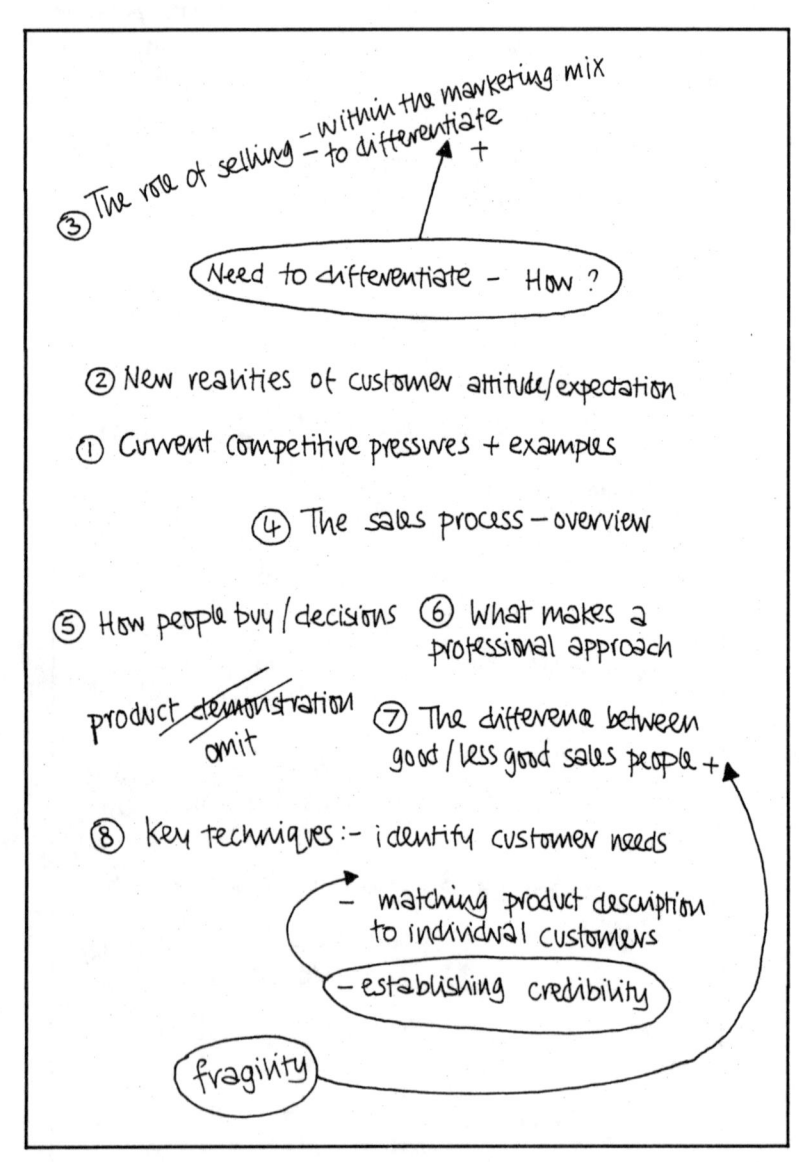

---

③ The role of selling – within the marketing mix – to differentiate

(Need to differentiate – How?)

② New realities of customer attitude/expectation

① Current competitive pressures + examples

④ The sales process – overview

⑤ How people buy/decisions   ⑥ What makes a professional approach

product ~~demonstration~~ omit   ⑦ The difference between good/less good sales people +

⑧ Key techniques:– identify customer needs
– matching product description to individual customers
– establishing credibility

(fragility)

(ii) Sorting

Next you can proceed to rearrange what you have written more logically. This may raise new questions as well as resolve others, so is still not a final structure. Such initial rearrangement may be best done by annotating the original list (a second colour is useful). Figure 3 continues the example started previously.

(iii) Arranging

Only now do you add (or redraft as your jottings may have become untidy and difficult to follow) the sequence and precise arrangement of the topic. Here the general principles are shown, the detail of exactly how you should view the structure of a talk forms the thread to the next chapter. This can be simply presented – see figure 4 – or be elaborated into the final form of whatever style of 'speaker's notes' for which you opt. Such notes can usefully add a note of any emphasis necessary in presenting the material – anything from a dramatic pause to a raised voice, or a point repeated for emphasis. More is said about this final form later (see page 38), here we concentrate on assembling the content of the message-to-be, as it were.

Note: two points are worth a special mention here:

- although a common early fear is that you will not have sufficient material, more often the reverse is true, and a common fault is trying to squeeze in too much, resulting in a rushed rather than a measured delivery and an audience missing much of what is there, or worse, becoming confused
- this limit on quantity is particularly true of individual points – there should not be too many – and the key skeleton of key points, and sub-points, should stand out and be manageable within the total material.

It is difficult to suggest a rule of thumb here. It is clearly dangerous to leave out a key element of an argument, but time is at a premium in most organizations these days and succinctness is often either appreciated, or essential. Having a clear structure

Figure 4. *Arranging: example of this stage of preparation*

The rough notes of the listing and sorting stages are now rewritten in an ordered form, which can be subject to final review as necessary:

---

1. Current competitive pressures – examples –
   –
   –

2. New realities of customer attitude/expectation

3. The role of selling – within the marketing mix
   – as a differentiating element for company product

4. The Sales Process: overview

5. How people make buying decisions

6. What makes for sales professionalism

7. Difference between good/less good sales people and fragility of process

8. Key techniques for success
   – identifying customer needs
   – establishing credibility
   – matching product description to individual customers

Note: this then becomes the main skeleton in terms of structure and content, dividing into a beginning, middle and end, and being fleshed out and turned into your own form of running notes to provide the level of detail required.

allows you to be sure the content is appropriate, matching that to the audience and to time restraints will help you make a final decision. If in doubt it is probably better to limit points rather than confuse with sheer quantity; leaving people wanting more may be better than boring them to death with seemingly endless minute detail.

(iv) Review

Finally, you need to review what you have done. It is no reflection on your abilities if it is not to your complete satisfaction first time. Many people need to work over material several times to get it right. At this stage it may suffice to check over what is down on paper in your mind, or you may want to go further and effectively *rehearse*. This too may be in your head, but may involve talking through the final form out loud. It may be worthwhile to practise to the bathroom mirror or have a trial run through with a sympathetic colleague (though on second thoughts you may think it prudent to omit the 'sympathetic'; some constructive criticism and ideas may well help, though you must ultimately decide the final form).

This final stage is important and can quickly fine-tune material into something that is not simply a sound message, but one arranged so that it can be effectively delivered.

The detail about making the presentation reviewed later will reinforce the need for careful preparation. There is a good deal to think about. But there is no reason why, with practice, the process should not be accomplished in a reasonable amount of time, but to begin with at least it should not be skimped. There is a good deal to think about, and even a short talk demands care and attention. (Some would say that one should say *especially* a short talk, and certainly in a few short minutes any fault will stand out sharply and small details can have a disproportionate impact for both good and ill; but I digress).

Next we turn to the manifestation of this preparation: speaker's notes. Few can sustain a well-organized talk without some written detail in front of them (though practice or repetition may allow you to reduce this in some instances to a few key words). Initially having something thought through that really suits you is vital, but it cannot be any old series of jottings. It must be tailored to its use.

Speaker's notes

Having something clear and simple to follow as a guide boosts confidence, it acts like a firm hand on the tiller, assisting you to maintain direction and aiding control (and also facilitating digression where appropriate). As has been said earlier the trick is not to write out the speech verbatim, rather to reflect the skeleton of the material, prompt particular inputs – from moments of emphasis, such as a dramatic pause, to using a visual of some sort – and to remind you of the detail against the background of a clear structure.

It is worth evolving a format that suits *you*. There is no need to follow anyone else's ideas unless they suit – though take what is useful from wherever you come across it. If you use the same broad approach consistently it speeds preparation and assists time-keeping as you get to know how long a page or card in your personal style represents.

The following comments are designed to help you develop such a style. Some practical points first:

- notes must be visible (use a sufficiently large size of type or writing)
- ensure they stay flat at the point you want (a A4 ring binder may be best, or cards loosely linked with a tie-cord)
- using only one side of the paper allows amendment and addition if necessary
- always number the pages – you do not want to get lost (and you would not be the first to drop notes if disaster strikes). Try doing the numbering in reverse, with the last page being number one – the countdown effect acts to provide information about how much material and time you have left in front of you as you proceed
- separate different kinds of instruction and material (e.g. what you will say and how you will say it)

- use colour and symbols to provide emphasis.

For example, imagine first a small segment of a presentation as it would be spoken in full. Here is a possible extract discussing, appropriately, speaker's notes:

> Even experienced speakers worry about losing their way. What's more there are, as you may have noticed, numerous other matters you may find worrying as well. Keeping track need not be one of them.
>
> Two main things are important here: preparation, which we have already discussed, and speaker's notes, which I will say a little about now. You need to develop a good system for creating the material you will have in front of you on the day. If you do, then it has real benefits. For instance, you won't lose your way. You will remember to show the next slide at the right moment and give different points the emphasis you want. Let's see how this works, and look at how much material you need to note down, the format that works best and how you get the key points to jump out at you.
>
> First, how detailed do notes need to be?

And so on, but this should provide enough for our purposes.

With these actual spoken words in mind, consider what might go down on the page. This is shown (overleaf). The detail here will be sufficient to give any speaker – who is otherwise prepared – something easy to follow. The grey tint represents the bright colour of a highlighter pen (use your imagination!). Certainly colour makes a difference to the clarity of these sorts of notes and can be used in numbers of ways: if underlining, bullet points, certain words, symbols etc. as well as highlighting stands out in, say, red, it does help. In this way the eye can quickly focus on each element without too much conscious effort.

Figure 5 uses a number of particular ideas you may be able to copy or adapt:

- the page is ruled (use colour here) into three smaller blocks that are each of a size that is easier to focus on as you look back from the audience to the page (remember the example represents an A4 page)

40 *Making Successful Presentations*

Figure 5. *Speaker's notes: format example*

	3.45 pm after tea	
SPEAKERS NOTES (S6)	(!) − lose way ? / + other worries − <u>no</u> need	+ example of difficulty ? tear

	* 1. preparation
	 2. speakers notes ↲
	  "Helps you (eg) - keep track
	      − next slide
	      − emphasis	

HOW?..	− quantity / detail − format − emphasis on key points (in turn) 📄	
QUANTITY		

Key: (S6) is the sixth slide. * always precedes key points.
↲ Links. You might use other symbols for emphasis (!)
pause (...) list points (📄), with underlining, capitals and
self-explanatory signs (like +) adding to your personal shorthand

- symbols are used (for example, here to show there is a slide, a need to pause etc.)
- columns, here separating main headings from the body of the notes and leaving room for additional material
- emphasis is shown (again colour is best)
- it is spaced out (to allow further amendment and make it easier to focus on)
- timing is mentioned
- the page is numbered
- there are options that can be used, or not, as time and circumstances allow, something that can be very useful to both timing and fine-tuning perhaps in light of a group's reaction.

Remember you should think carefully about what suits you best and evolve a personal style that works for you; it is worth a little experiment. The end result can be typed, or handwritten, or a mixture of both.

This is an area worth thinking about and experimenting with. You will find that if you decide on a style of reminder note that really suits you, it provides a real asset to you thereafter. The style may evolve over time, you may have different versions of it for differing purposes, and the amount of detail may be different depending on how well you know the topic on which you must present. It will always act as a sure foundation to what you have to do and its very familiarity will, in time, become a part of its usefulness.

Now, well prepared and with your notes ready you can consider the detail of exactly how you will put the material across.

With a little help from your friends

Before leaving the subject of preparation, there is the matter of team presentations to be touched on. When *the* presentation is made up of segments with perhaps two, three or more people contributing segments of it, the need for preparation is magnified. Team presentations must appear *seamless*. There should be neither any disruption to the smooth flow of the content, nor any fumbling in terms of handover between speakers. Any uncertainty will be read by the group as unprofessional, and either a sign of bad planning or lack of respect for the audience; or both.

It is extremely difficult for a group of people to present effectively together without getting together beforehand to thrash out the details. Time and pressures within many an organization may typically conspire to make such meetings difficult; but there is no substitute for them. A word or two on the telephone is just not the same.

You need to consider such matters as:

- what order you will speak in (and whether this in any way should relate to the hierarchy involved, often it should not)
- who is 'in charge'
- who leads
- how speaking styles match or detract
- who will take questions
- the implications for the timing

and more.

It is worth a moment. The effect of a seamless ultimate presentation is powerful. It is no fun getting up to speak less well prepared than you know you should be, getting up alongside a colleague having little idea how what the two of you will say will mesh runs a close second.

A final thought

Most, if not all of the problems you may anticipate can be removed or reduced by preparation. It can quite literally make the difference between success and failure, and can turn something routine into something memorable. Psychologists say that more than seventy per cent of what is called 'self-talk' about presenting is negative; all those thoughts that start: 'I'm not sure I can . . .' or 'It won't be . . .'. You need to combat this positively. Imagine it going well. Visualize the detail of particular elements working. Doubts might otherwise become a self-fulfilling prophecy.

The time for this thinking is as you prepare. What you do in preparing creates the certainty it *will* go well.

Prepare – practise – present.

A final rule

Set time aside to – *excuse me, I'm just – well, just a minute* Now, yes – set aside time to – *sorry to interrupt but* – Where was I? A final rule:

Try to set aside time to prepare or rehearse uninterrupted. It makes for a quicker and more certain job in the end. Something done piecemeal will make creating a fluid whole more difficult.

4 Putting it Over

> Speeches are like babies – easy
> to conceive but hard to deliver
> Pat O'Malley

Presentations should have a beginning, a middle and an end. The oldest, and perhaps the wisest, saying about communications generally is the advice to: Tell 'em, tell 'em and tell 'em. In other words you should tell people what you are going to tell them, tell them and then tell them what you have told them (it is the way, for instance a good written report is arranged: introduction, the body of the content and a summary). If this sounds common sense, it is. It is also the most useful basis on which to approach a presentation for both speaker and audience alike. It works. The lack of it is also a common fault. I regularly see people who in other ways are good presenters, diluting the impression they make because they are following no clear structure. Their audience gets lost or finds what is being said difficult to follow and they end up being less impressive than they would be if what they did had such a structure.

So, practising what I preach I will link that thought to another and say, briefly, how this chapter is arranged. First, it is no good there being a structure if people are unaware of it, so the topic of what is called *signposting* is dealt with next. This leads us to some thoughts about *the audience*, the group to whom everything discussed in this book is ultimately directed. Then the stages – beginning, middle and end – are reviewed in turn to investigate both how they can be made to form a cohesive whole and also how the detailed way they are handled can make them successful in putting your ideas over.

First then, back to signposting.

Signposting

The technique of signposting (or, as it is sometimes called, labelling) is something that can be used throughout the presentation process. As people like knowing broadly what they are in for, and appreciate – albeit perhaps subconsciously – help in keeping everything well ordered and in context, then this is an important technique in carrying a group with you. Indeed, it simply cannot be overdone. It consists simply of telling people, in outline or in brief, not only what is coming next, but sometimes the purpose or texture of it as well.

It can start with the whole talk. You spell out what is, in effect, an agenda. Thus in talking about a project of some sort, you might say: 'Today I want to review three key issues. First, what needs to be done, second, who will do what, and third, the timing . . .' If the presentation is of any length or complexity, then a similar technique can precede and lead into sub-points: 'Now second I said I would discuss the audience; here I want to mention two main, and different, perspectives – what they expect and what they need. First, expectations . . .'. Exactly the same sort of process may be relevant down several layers. One point, and something I know I must watch; keep count. I am apt to say, authoritatively: 'There are four key issues here' and when I am up to six, someone in the group will take delight in pointing out that I cannot count (I reply that I *can* count and it is my creativity that is providing the additional key points).

This is not simply a convenient device to keep yourself organized, though it does have that effect. People like it. They like to have things in context, know clearly how one thing links to another and know – in advance – something about what is coming next. Similarly you can flag or label the exact nature of particular things you say:

- *specifically*: 'Now let me give you an example . . .': an example is coming
- *by implication*: 'For instance . . .': there is probably an example coming
- *with added meaning*: 'This is an odd way of looking at it, but

makes a point . . .': an example is probably coming and it is not a routine one, might even be amusing
- *with added content*: 'Consider this in relation to, for instance, an elephant . . .': an example coming up extends the content to a new, and perhaps, unexpected area
- *with an obvious flourish*: 'You may think that's irrelevant. In fact it's not an elephant, it's a hippopotamus . . .': the example is used as a pace-breaking aside with a touch of humour (well, when my children were younger we all thought it was funny).

In this way the wording you use can signpost intention in all sorts of ways. You can tell people to: pay particular attention to a complex point, to relax, relate what is being said to their experience in some way, or answer (a perhaps rhetorical) question that you will soon pose. It can get them thinking along particular lines, adding elements of their own experience to support an argument, or just prompt them to file away one point and turn their mind to consideration of the next. With that in mind, consider (signpost!) what the audience want.

The audience

As has been said earlier the audience want it all to go well. But they are not totally forgiving and they will have expectations; above all they want you to talk *to* them or *discuss with* them, not to talk *at* them. So keeping the audience viewpoint in mind is, like preparation, another near 'magic' formula for success. It is one that should, of course, affect your preparation as well as your delivery and manner.

Any audience faced with being on the receiving end of a presentation thinks ahead – a process that may perhaps be coloured by experience of bad or boring presentations they have attended in the past – trying to guess what it will be like. They wonder if it will be interesting, amusing, useful; or short. Whatever the intended intention is, they wonder if it will be achieved. They look for clues to what it will be like even before you start, which is why things like appearance, starting on time, being seen to be organized and comfortable with the proceedings are all important. In training for instance, people are asking questions such as: does the trainer know his subject? will they be able to put it over? and do so in an interesting manner, and, if they do, will it help me? Each member of a group is an individual, they are concerned above all with themselves, and the good presenter appears to address individuals not some amorphous creature called 'audience'.

More specifically, *they want* you:

- to 'know your stuff'
- to look the part
- to respect them and acknowledge their situation and views
- to find what you say links to what they want from the talk
- to be given sufficient information to make a considered judgement about what you say (they will weigh up your views, especially if they are going to be required to take some action at the end or after the presentation ends)
- to understand by the end what that action, if any, is

and, above all they want to find it *understandable, interesting* and *a good fit* with the audience and the occasion.

Conversely, *they do not want* to be:

- confused
- blinded with science, technicalities or jargon
- 'lost' in the structure (or lack of it)
- talked down to
- made to struggle to understand inappropriate language
- made to make an enormous jump to relate what is said to their own circumstance

and they do not want to listen to someone whose lack of preparation makes it clear that they have no respect for the group.

You have to earn their attention, however, create a belief in your credentials for talking to them, create a rapport between yourself and the group, make them want to listen and understand – yet perhaps also keep an open mind throughout about what is still to come. Presentation is aided by a healthy amount of empathy on the part of the speaker and you can do a lot worse than think long and hard about any audience you are due to address; the more you know about them the better, and some prior checking is sometimes advisable. If you expect the group to be very different, in age or experience say, from what is in fact the case, there is a strong likelihood that some at least of what you say to them will fall on stony ground.

Now, as promised, we turn to the overall structure and start, with certain logic, at the beginning.

A good start

One cannot overestimate the importance of a good start. Remember the old saying: *first impressions last*. The beginning is the introduction; it must set the scene, state the topic and theme (and maybe the reason for it) – and do so clearly, *and* begin to get into the 'meat' of the message, and do so without too much delay. But it cannot do this in a vacuum. It must get the group's attention and carry people along – and link into the middle and the main section and message of the talk. And to do all this it must establish some sort of rapport between the speaker and audience, one that must become an acceptable basis for holding the interest on through the presentation. Consider attention and rapport in turn.

Gaining attention

Two things assist here, your manner and the actual start you make. Your manner must get people saying to themselves: 'This should be interesting – I think they know what they are talking about'. Here a confident manner pays dividends. If you look the part and proceed as if you are sure of yourself then they will take it you are. The assumption is you would not be doing the talking if you did not know your stuff. But if you appear hesitant or ill prepared then they will start to worry, and that normal assumption will evaporate.

Exactly what you say first is also important. Not so much any formalities (though you could turn 'Good morning' or 'Ladies and Gentlemen' into something more grabbing), but the first real statement or point. Some examples of opening techniques you might consider follow:

- *news*: something you know they do not know (and will want to): 'Gentlemen, we have hit the target. I heard just as I came into the meeting and . . .'
- *a question*: actual or rhetorical and ideally designed to get people responding (at least in their minds): 'How would you like to . . .'
- *a quotation*: whether famous or what a member of the group said yesterday, if it makes a point, generates a smile or links firmly to the topic this can work well: 'It was Oscar Wilde who said: "There is only one thing in the world worse than being talked about, and that is not being talked about"' (used to introduce the public relations plan, perhaps)
- *a story or anecdote*: perhaps again to make a point, maybe something people know: 'We all remember the moment when the . . .', or something they do not: 'Last week in Singapore I got caught in the rain and . . .'
- *a fact*: preferably a striking one; or maybe challenging, provoking or surprising: 'Research shows that if we give a customer cause to complain, they are likely to tell ten other people, but if we please them they will only tell one. Not a ratio to forget because . . .'
- *drama*: something that surprises or shocks, or in some way delivers a punch: 'The next ten minutes can change your life. It can . . .'
- *a gesture*: something people watch and which gets their attention: 'Some people in this company seem to think that money grows on trees' *said while tearing up a bank note*
- *history*: this may be a general historical fact or one that evokes a common memory: 'During 1992, when we all knew the company was at a turning point . . .'
- *curiosity*: an oddity, something that will surprise and have people waiting (eagerly) for the link with what is going to be said – it may be really odd or just out of context: 'Now you may wonder why I should start with a reference to pachyderms; you may even wonder what it is.' (It is a thick-skinned quadruped; utterly irrelevant . . .)
- *silence*: this may seem a contradiction in terms; but *can* be used: 'Please all remain absolutely quiet for a moment – *the speaker*

counts silently to ten and the gap begins to seem rather long – that's how long it seems to customers waiting for Technical Support to answer the telephone; and it is too long'
- *a checklist*: this can spell out what is coming and there are certainly worse starts than that: 'There are four key issues I want to raise today. They are . . .'.

Such devices are not mutually exclusive. They may be used in a variety of combinations and the list is not exhaustive; you may well be able to think of more. Whatever you use, and the impact may come from several sentences rather than something as short as the examples used above, the first words need careful preparation and must be delivered to achieve exactly the effect you are after.

Creating rapport

The creation of rapport is not subsidiary to gaining interest; the two may be inextricably bound up. Think of anything you can build in that will foster group feeling, for example:

- be careful of personal pronouns. There are moments to say 'you' and others for 'we' (and sometimes fewer for 'I'). Thus 'We should consider . . .' may well be better than 'You must . . .' or 'I think you should . . .'
- use a (careful) compliment or two: 'As experienced people you will . . .'
- use words that reinforce your position or competence (not to boast, but to imply you belong to the group): 'Like you I have to travel a great deal. I know the problems it makes with continuity in the office . . .'
- be *enthusiastic*, but always genuinely so (this reminds me of the awful American expression that *if you can fake the sincerity, then everything else is easy*; back to enthusiasm). Real enthusiasm implies sincerity and both may be needed. Expressing enthusiasm tends to automatically make you more animated and, another saying: *enthusiasm is the only good thing that is infectious.*

At the same time as the factors mentioned here being important, there are also specific tasks to achieve in this first stage of the presentation. Again there may be a number of such tasks, by way of example the following are often high on the list to:

- describe/define the topic
- state the objective
- say why this is necessary
- tell them something about the structure
- say enough to catch their interest (not just for the moment, but in what is coming)
- start, if necessary, to be seen to satisfy expectations
- show why what you are doing is relevant – *to them*
- encourage, if necessary, the audience to keep an open mind
- reinforce (good) early first impressions (of yourself and the event).

The manner of delivery, emphasis and so on clearly contribute also to the effectiveness of this, indeed every, stage and therefore to how you get its message across. But perhaps most important of all the beginning sets the scene for the audience. They begin to judge how it is going in their terms, so if they:

- feel it is beginning to be accurately directed at them
- feel their specific needs are being considered and respected
- feel the speaker is engaging
- begin to identify with what is being said ('that's right')

then you will have them with you and can proceed to the main segment of the presentation – with confidence that a good reaction at the start can be a firm foundation for continuing success.

But the beginning is by its nature brief. It may be a few sentences or a few minutes. Certainly it should not unbalance the rest; you cannot spend twenty minutes leading up to two minutes and two points of content. Whatever the kind of presentation you give, it may be useful to note the percentage of the total duration which is effectively the beginning, and plan accordingly. Important though it is there is perhaps even more hanging on the next stage.

The middle – and the main message

This is the main part of the presentation and it is probably also the longest. During this stage there is the greatest need for organization of the message and for clarity of purpose. Your key aims should be to:

- put over the detail of the message
- maintain attention and interest
- do so clearly and in a manner appropriate to the audience

and, if necessary, to seek acceptance and, conversely, avoid people actively disagreeing with what you say. (It is not always necessary to aim for agreement, but this is often the intention and may well be the prime objective.)

Given the length and greater complexity of the middle segment, it is important for it to be well ordered. This includes the simple procedure of taking one point at a time. Here again I will try to practise what I preach, the following points will help this segment go well.

Putting over the content

This needs:

- *a logical sequence*: for example discussing a process in chronological order
- *the use of what are effectively plenty of main and sub-headings*: this is, in part, what was referred to earlier as signposting: 'There are three key points here: performance, method and cost. Let's take performance first . . .' It gives advance warning of what is coming and keeps the whole message from becoming rambling and difficult to follow because of it
- *clarity*: people must understand what you say. There must be no verbosity. Not too much jargon. No convoluted arguments and no awkward turns of phrase. This is as much a question of words as of elements of greater length. Not only must there be no manual excavation devices, you must call a spade a spade and, should you actually speak of spades, they need to be relevant and interesting spades.

Note: never underestimate the need for care if you are to achieve prompt and clear understanding. Communications can be inherently difficult. You need to make sure that there is a considerable probability of a degree of definite cognition amongst those various different people in the audience; sorry – that everyone will easily understand what you say (see figure 6).

KISS

To help understanding:
Keep **I**t **S**imple, **S**peaker
or, as some put it less politely: Keep It Simple, Stupid.

- Short words
- Short sentences
- Short paragraphs (sections)
- No more jargon than is appropriate
- Clarity of explanation
- Description that paints a picture
- Signpost intentions
- Group topics/points (groups of three to four work well; think how you remember a telephone number in short units)

Figure 6. *KISS*

Some examples expand the point:

- certain phrases are not only convoluted, they can be annoying. Among a few that come to mind are: *at this moment in time* – when what is meant is now, or *in the not too distant future* – when soon would be better

- the use of totally unnecessary words: *basically* – at the start of a sentence, or unnecessary fashionable words like everything currently being *proactive* (what is wrong with active?) when for instance it would be better to say: 'a response' rather than *a proactive response*
- inadvertently giving a wrong impression, either by being vague: *quite nice* – applied, say, to a person does it mean they are good to know or is it merely being polite? Or by being imprecise: a *continuous process* – might just be continual, for instance, depending on whether it is without interval or never ending. You can doubtless think of more, it is sometimes surprising how loosely language is used, and in a formal situation you often do not receive any feedback or know that a false interpretation has been taken on board. You can never therefore think too carefully about exactly how you put things
- be descriptive: with language (e.g. smooth as silk, not shiny); with similes (say 'It is like . . .' as often as you can think of good allusions). Examples are also important here. It is one thing to say, 'This is a change that will be straightforward and cause no problems', perhaps with the group thinking to themselves that if you expect them to believe that you will be selling them Tower Bridge next. It is quite another to say: 'This is a change that will be straightforward and cause no problem' and then link it to something else: 'It will be very like when the company's appraisal system changed, there were plenty of fears about exactly what would happen, but the system and the training worked well. I don't think any of us would prefer the old ways' – though of course the example must be appropriate (it would be no good in the example just given if the introduction of the new appraisal system was regarded as being a disaster)
- *be careful not to make wrong assumptions*: about people's level of knowledge, understanding, degree of past experience or existing views for instance, or what you say based on them will not hit home
- *use visual aids*: a picture is worth a thousand words, they say,

and checklists and exhibits – and more – are all a real help in getting the message across; let them speak for themselves (pause in speaking when you first show something – attention cannot be simultaneously on what you are saying and the visual) and make sure they support what you are doing rather than become the lead element – more of this in Chapter Six

- *include gestures*: let your physical manner add emphasis, an appropriate feel and variety
- *make your voice work*: in the sense that your tone makes it clear whether you are serious, excited, enthusiastic or any other emotion or emphasis you wish to bring to bear in this way, as well as watching as it were the mechanics of the voice (speaking at the right volume and pace, for instance).

Note: a number of the above aspects, such as voice, which may appear to have been commented on only briefly here are returned to and expanded on in the next chapter.

So far so good, but there is more to be achieved than just putting over the content. You may well want people to agree with your ideas.

Gaining acceptance

This too can be assisted in a number of ways:

- *relating to the specific group*: general points and argument may not be so readily accepted as those carefully tailored to the nature and experience of a specific audience. (With some topics this is best interpreted as describing how things will affect *them* or what they will do for *them*)
- *provide proof*: certainly if acceptance is desired, you need to offer something other than your word – as the speaker you may very well be seen as having a vested interest in your own ideas. Thus adding opinion, references or tests from elsewhere and preferably from a respected and/or comparable source strengthens your case

Note: it is particularly important not to forget *feedback* during this important stage:

- *watch* for signs (nodding, fidgeting, whispered conversation, and just expressions) as to how your message is going down – try to scan the whole audience (you need in any case to maintain good eye contact around the group)
- *listen* too for signs – a restless audience, for example, has its own unmistakable sound
- *ask* for feedback. There are certainly many presentations where asking questions of the group is perfectly acceptable, and it may be expected – even a brief show of hands may assist you
- *aim* to build in answers to objections you may feel will be in the audience's mind, either mentioning the fact: 'I know what you are thinking; it can't be done in the time. Well, I believe it can. Let me tell you how . . .'. Or by not making a specific mention, but simply building in information intended to remove fears.

Even if you build in answers to likely disagreement, some may still surface.

When you have completed the main thrust of your message then you can move towards the end.

The end

Perhaps this first point here relates to a moment before the end. So be it, it is worth a mention. Good time-keeping is impressive. But it is not assumed. So flagging that the end is in sight may be useful, though you should allude reasonably specifically to what that means. If it is not just two more sentences, say so: 'Right, I have two more points to make and then perhaps I may take a couple of minutes to summarize' – 'With five minutes of my time remaining, I would like to . . .'. This is just signposting again, but if it engenders a feeling which says something like: 'My goodness, they look like finishing right on time', then that can be good.

Having said that, what are the requirements of a good ending? Two things predominate:

- a pulling together
- ending on a high note

But first, consider some dangers.

An ending that goes less than just right can be noticed disproportionately by the audience; and, at worst, it can spoil the whole thing. Beware of the following:

- *false endings*: there should be one ending (preferably flagged once); if you say '. . . and finally . . .' three or four times then people understandably find it irritating
- *wandering*: an end that never seems to actually arrive, though what is being said constantly makes it sound imminent
- *second speech*: a digression, particularly a lengthy one, may be inappropriate close to the end when the audience are expecting everything to be promptly wrapped up
- *a rush to the finishing line*: this is a danger when time is pressing, it may be better to say you will overrun by a few minutes or abbreviate earlier if time is running away from you than find yourself gabbling in a race to reach the finishing time
- *repetition*: or at least unnecessary repetition (for summary is another matter), is something else that can distract towards the close.

With that in mind we turn to the positive. Summary is not the easiest thing to do succinctly and accurately. Hence if it is well done then it can be impressive. Consider this in another context, that of a written report. If, after reading twenty pages, you come to three paragraphs at the end that pull the whole thing neatly together and do so effectively, then you think better of the whole document (in addition, people who find summary difficult respect those who do it well). So for presentations (and for reports, for that matter) this is something that is well worth careful preparation.

A pulling together or summary is a logical conclusion, it may link to the action you hope people will take following the presentation or simply present the final point. Whatever it contains the ending should be comparatively brief. Having made the final point – with all the other factors now referred to continuing to be important throughout this stage – you need to end with something of a flourish.

That said, it is worth mentioning that your final words should never (or at least very rarely) be 'Thank you'. It is not that a thank you is not appropriate, it may well be essential, but that it makes a poor last word. What happens is that the talk appears to tail away, a final punchy point being apt to be followed by something like: 'Well, perhaps I should end with a thank you, it has been a pleasure to be here. Thank you very much.' It is much better to have the thank you *before* the final point: 'Thank you for being here, I am grateful for your attention. Now, a final word in conclusion . . .'.

That final word may need to be based on some simple technique (rather like the opening, so only a few examples are given here):

- *a question*: maybe repeating an opening question, maybe leaving something hanging in the air, maybe with the intention of prolonging the time people continue to think about the topic
- *a quotation*: particularly the sort that encapsulates a thought briefly
- *a story*: allowing more time to put over a concluding point
- *an injunction to act*: where appropriate: 'So, go out and . . .'.

However you finish remember that your last remarks will linger in the mind a little more than much of what went before. If you want to make people think, for instance, then your final words will act as a major part of what allows you to succeed in that aim.

At the end of the day, when you sit down or later back in your office (or over a large gin and tonic! – which incidentally is when you should have it; a drink before a presentation 'to steady the nerves' is not recommended, and too much may loosen your inhibitions to the point where your tongue takes on a life of its own), what do you want? For the audience to:

- have had their expectations met (perhaps, better still, surpassed)

- have understood
- have followed the detail, logic and technicality of any argument you have been promoting
- warmed to you as a speaker (and felt whatever you may have wished to project, for example, trust or belief in your expertise)
- seen what was done and how it was done as appropriate to them

and found the whole thing interesting, stimulating or . . . the adjective needs to reflect the circumstances and intention.

You may not feel, at this stage, that you will ever look forward to making a presentation. But you are certainly likely to find that you can fairly quickly come to enjoy the feeling of having *made* one that has gone as you wished, and find that one that has gone really well produces real satisfaction for both the audience and the speaker. And, who knows, if you follow all the advice here you may even begin to find that as well as becoming more certain of the process and, as a result, doing a better job on it, you do begin to draw some pleasure from it.

The principles reviewed in this chapter and the thread of the way a clear structure is used are a major part of all the influences that can make a presentation effective. But there is more to it then that. A variety of tricks of the trade as it were can also help to increase the certainty of your meeting your objectives precisely. It is to these that we turn in the next chapter.

5 Tricks of the Trade

> A speaker who does not strike oil
> in ten minutes should stop boring
> *Louis Nizer*

Though it may provide a place for it, structure cannot inject a sparkle. Having dealt with the overall structure in the last chapter, here we turn to how manner and behaviour can inject additional meaning, emphasis and feeling into a presentation. The factors mentioned here necessarily form a varied list as the process is dissected. No apology for that, it is the nature of the subject. Further it should be clear at the outset that the factors discussed are not mutually exclusive. One of the complexities of the overall process is that there is a good deal happening at one and the same time. This means that there is much to think about at the same time. A clear understanding of the processes involved and the development of the right reflexes and habits are important to an ability to orchestrate the whole, and to fine-tuning as the presentation moves along.

Everything that follows is important because people do a lot more than listen. They *experience* a presentation. Everything about the manner and demeanour of the speaker contributes to the overall feeling they take away. And non-verbal factors are as important as verbal ones. How you look has already been mentioned; here we start with how you *look*.

Using your eyes

Eye contact with the members of the group makes an important contribution to the overall way in which a speaker is perceived. Here we review how you can maximize the impact you make in this respect. Consider first what constitutes good eye contact. Overall two factors are particularly important:

- it should be comprehensive, taking in all of the group (or all parts of a large audience) and continue throughout the presentation
- it should be deliberate and noticeable (this means that eye contact must be maintained for longer than would be normal in ordinary conversation – perhaps for periods of four to five seconds rather than two to three).

Thus it is very much something that can only become truly effective once it becomes a habit, and it is a habit which you must work to acquire. To digress for a moment, everything of this sort may seem a little daunting initially. If you can remember learning to drive, then the same probably applied. To begin with certain aspects of the process seemed virtually physically impossible, but soon, almost without you realizing it, they became habits. Thus something such as checking your rear view mirror at certain points as you drive become all but automatic. In presenting there are numbers of things that will acquire similar characteristics and eye contact is certainly one. Initially, however, you need to work at it becoming more automatic, and later at responding to it when appropriate. After all there is no point in scanning the group if you learn nothing from it, and if it appears too automatic then it will have a less positive effect on the group, who after all want to feel you are interested in them.

On the other hand, consider what *bad* eye contact – looking too long at your notes, away from the group (into the corner of the room or out of the window), or at one or two favoured members of the group to the exclusion of the others – can lead to. It can mean:

- no, or poor, rapport with the audience
- giving an impression of being anxious, nervous or, at worst, incompetent
- an impression of lack of sincerity
- reduced credibility
- the speaker obtaining little or no feedback
- the presentation faltering (especially because of any lack of feedback)
- no opportunity for certain kinds of fine-tuning as the talk proceeds based on feedback. For example: feedback might

show incomprehension of some point which can then be elaborated (something to watch for particularly with technical points and figures).

Contrast this with *good* eye contact – which shows the speaker is in touch with the audience – can give an impression which produces a number of benefits:

- it establishes rapport with the group, which demonstrates you care about them and increases their belief that the presentation will be right for them
- this interest in the group increases credibility, trust and attention
- the speaker appears more confident, more assertive, more professional, more expert (it can enhance any intended feeling of this sort)
- it allows feedback (it is useful to know if people appear attentive, interested, supportive or bored or indifferent)
- such feedback can be used to fine-tune the detail of what is being done
- all positive benefits felt by the speaker act in some way to build confidence which, in turn, helps improve what is being done.

For example, a speaker trying to put over something difficult or contentious will find their manner (and perhaps use of feedback) contributes much to achieving their aims, or vice versa.

Watch here for, and avoid, any automatic pattern developing. It is disconcerting for an audience to see a speaker going through a routine of looking at each section of the group in, say, a clockwise circuit. Remember that good eye contact is a habit to foster (and you will not develop exactly what you want perfectly instantly). Remember too that if the speaker is:

- well prepared
- familiar with their material
- working from clear notes (that do not need lengthy attention to spot what comes next)
- comfortable in their environment
- relaxed and confident

> **Try it**
>
> It may be useful to conduct a short exercise with yourself to demonstrate and develop this technique. Present for a minute or two in front of a mirror, *without speaking out loud or worrying about exactly what is being said* (you can follow a planned preparation in mind and with notes in front of you if necessary). This allows greater concentration to go on what the eyes should be doing and greater emphasis can be given to this aspect. Watch your face and see how your eyes are moving.
>
> Concentration on any one factor amongst many, isolating it for attention will always help you fine-tune exactly how a particular aspect of the process is being utilized.

their ability to produce good eye contact is enhanced.

Next we consider the more obvious speaker's asset; the voice.

Using your voice

The first step towards maximizing what can be done with the voice is to be relaxed and project it effectively, something we touched on in reviewing how to overcome nerves. The voice has an almost infinite capacity to vary meaning and emphasis, not just with regard to what is said but also how. Often tiny changes in tone can vary meaning. Consider a simple sentence with the emphasis placed on particular words:

- It is your *voice* that makes the difference
- It is *your* voice that makes the difference

or the slight difference that puts a question mark at the end of a sentence:

- You are not sure
- You are not sure?

or the two together:

- You are *not* sure?

So the voice needs to be used in two key ways. It must be clearly audible, and it must have variety – varying pace and pitch – to produce a suitable emphasis. Here we review the way in which this occurs and consider ways of achieving what you want from your voice.

It is always something of a shock to the system for people to hear themselves (on video in training sessions it may be see and hear). Your voice is perhaps a particular shock, no one *ever* hears themselves as others hear them unless they are recorded. Some faults, such as talking too fast (often an effect of nerves), can be quickly corrected once people have heard how they really sound.

> **Try it**
>
> Try recording a minute or two of your voice as a test. If you have not heard yourself recently it may be a shock, but recent exposure to how you *actually* sound is certainly useful if you feel you want to make any changes to the way you come over.

Two further points about the voice are important: audibility and emphasis.

Audibility

For the less experienced speaker, judging whether you will be heard clearly at the back of the room is a worry, but audibility is largely only in fact a matter of speaking somewhat louder than is usual in conversation. The simplest rule is to *direct what you say at the most distant part of the room* (keep the people in the back row in mind). It is important to get this right – a test was suggested earlier – clearly if people cannot actually hear you this is the ultimate problem, however hearing with a struggle is also dangerous, and will change the audience's view of you. The results may include the following:

- audience tends to become irritated
- audience attention is less on the message than on struggling to hear
- the speaker may well be regarded as nervous, inconsiderate, inexpert or worse
- a low voice tends also to be monotonous and thus boring.

On the other hand, a good clear delivery has advantages which are the antithesis of the above, giving a positive impression of the speaker as competent and commanding attention.

In addition, speaking up tends to be one factor which helps inject more animation and enthusiasm into a presentation. It encourages the speaker to use gestures and generally affects the professional way in which they come over.

Emphasis

The use of the voice to inject emphasis and animation to what you do is vital. A presentation that is put over in a lively and animated tone of voice, that *sounds* interesting and which varies its pace and pitch, will always go over better than one that is delivered on some kind of monotone.

Here we review a number of seemingly simple issues that contribute to making up the total impression of your message and *how* it goes over. We start with the reverse of voice: no voice at all.

PAUSES

What is *not* said is just as important as what is said. The pause can do a number of things:

- allow what has just been said to sink in
- give time for the audience to interpret or analyse what has been said (in the way that a rhetorical question can prompt thought)
- focus attention on something other than what is said (as with a visual aid)
- add drama (hence the 'dramatic pause')

- provide 'punctuation' (making a real break to separate one point from another)

and, not least, *give the speaker time to think.*

There is however a real difficulty with pauses – everyone thinks that they may overdo it and that it will turn into an embarrassment. This is a feeling that the instigator of a pause feels much more deeply than others, and that a formal speaker feels more acutely than members of the group addressed.

Try it

You can demonstrate this to yourself very simply: ask someone to help you with a short experiment, simply ask them to bear with you a moment and then count to ten slowly to yourself. Ask them what they think was the duration of the pause. It is likely to seem longer to them; indeed just counting ten slowly may seem to you to take an age. Time is relative.

Practise also saying a sentence that you know needs a pause within it. Say it several times varying the length of the pause to vary the effect. A tape recorder will make this and other exercises that much more revealing and useful.

If you need to pause and are worried about it becoming too long, or know you cannot judge the length you want, the solution is simple. You literally count silently to yourself (do not worry, no one will know!). In so doing you can take advantage of the fact that a pause can do a number of the things mentioned above and add something to your presentation. Because of its importance you may find it useful to have a prompt – a dotted line may suffice – to pausing in your note.

Next, let us return to what you do say.

WORDS

You cannot speak without using words, but what is important

here is how your exact choice of words can make a real – distinct – great – considerable – powerful – pronounced – difference to the totality of the message that you put over. This is sufficiently important to make having a thesaurus to hand during preparation very useful. A poor choice of words is easy to make, perhaps compounded by any nerves you may be experiencing, and is a common cause of presentations not being as effective as they might be. Sometimes the problem here is less one of incorrect thinking, and thus selection, than of not thinking at all. In other words, the first word that comes to mind may well not be the best for the circumstances. The audience must be a major factor in your selection, dictating, for example, what degree of technicality may be appropriate, as well as a straightforward level and style of language.

Consider the difference one word can make to meaning and emphasis, for instance in the sentence that follows:

The choice of words makes a *real* difference to the effect they have on a group.

> ### Try it
>
> Take a number of sentences, perhaps from a presentation you have made or must make, and try substituting alternatives to seek more precise meaning. If you take a bland word to start with it will lead you most easily into the process. To set you off try replacing the bland word *big* in the following:
>
> Improving my presentations skills could make a *big* difference in my job.
>
> What word might imply a difference in your ability to *do* something useful or important and do it effectively? – *significant* or *practical* perhaps?
>
> Try again picking your own sentences.

What if one of the following replaced *real?*: *distinct*; *great*; *considerable*; *powerful*; *pronounced*. Which sounds strongest? Think of the different contexts in which you would want different meanings for this: *powerful* to suggest that what is said carries influence, *pronounced* perhaps when the need is greater technical accuracy or precision.

You can apply exactly the same sort of thinking to phrases. For example, continuing the example above: 'Improving my presentations skills *will make me better able to tackle important parts of my job*' has a much more specific meaning than: 'Improving my presentations skill *will be very helpful*'.

Try it

This procedure can be repeated again focusing on:
– bland words or phrases (big, very, nice)
– cliches, and meaningless words or phrases (due to the fact that – when you mean: because)
– superfluous elements (sentences that begin 'Basically, ...)

and on words and sentences. Experimenting with the differences you can make, and your ability to find words and phrases that match the precise nuance you want, will lead to a more certainly expressive style.

Ultimately you have to select not simply the right word or phrase, but a well selected flow of words throughout the presentation. Perhaps more important than anything is clarity of meaning, linked perhaps with description which is pleasing as well as useful in conjuring up a picture. The boxed paragraph above provides an additional digression on this key aspect of putting the message across. The words and phrases you use must be well chosen, but they do not, on their own, do the complete job.

SOUNDS

How words are said is just as important as what they are. A variety of factors – the pitch of the voice, articulation, inflection and the emphasis given to particular words or phrases (or sentences for that matter) – are all instrumental in achieving your exact intended meaning. These are worth a separate word each:

- *Pitch*: this is the note – higher or lower – of your voice. Extremes away from the norm may add emphasis, and, of course, be coupled with other factors: for example saying something slower and lower can add a note of gravity. This is particularly important where you want to give the impression of such factors as importance, impatience, excitement or interest. Imagine the way the strength of a negative is affected by the pitch, if it sounds too light it may be taken to mean 'maybe', yet it can also be said in a way that unmistakably means NO.
- *Articulation*: this is the clarity of sound you put into what you say. If you mumble, something that is compounded by going at too fast a pace, you will not be understood. Even if you are, it is a strain for the listeners. They will not like it and may miss things as they struggle to keep up. Some things need particular clarity, for example:

- figures (you may not want 15% mistaken for 50%)
- Fs and Ss
- the sound at the end of words.

Before anything else, meaning must be clear. This may well seem obvious, but still you may benefit from double checking your clarity using a tape recorder: see figure 7 on page 72.

- *Inflection*: this is the way differing sound can add an additional meaning to a phrase (in the way that there may be a clear sound that implies a question mark follows a word – this can be important, for example a rhetorical question must be clearly recognizable to have its effect). This links closely to the next item below.

Getting to the nub of the message

The job of the speaker is to actively select a method of delivery that allows the true meaning and desription to shine through, making it easy, noticeably easy, for the audience to understand.

Business communication often springs from habits and style that obscure the meaning. The much quoted 'standard progress report' (reproduced here as it appears in my book *Agreed!* [Kogan Page] is a spoof of the kind of writing that is all too common in business circles.

Standard Progress Report

For Those with No Progress to Report

During the survey period which ends 14 February, considerable progress has been made in the preliminary work directed towards the establishment of the initial activities. [*We are getting ready to start, but we have not done anything yet.*] The background information has been surveyed and the functional structure of the component parts of the cognizant organization has been clarified [*We looked at the project and decided that George would lead it.*]

Considerable difficulty has been encountered in the selection of optimum approaches and methods but this problem is being attacked vigorously and we expect the development phase will proceed at a satisfactory rate [*George is looking through the handbook*]. In order to prevent unnecessary duplication of previous efforts in the same field, it was necessary to establish a survey team which has conducted a rather extensive tour through various departments with immediate access to the system [*George and Harry had a nice time visiting everyone*].

The Steering Committee held its regular meeting and considered rather important policy matters pertaining to the overall organizational levels of the line and staff responsibilities that devolve on the personnel associated with the specific assignments resulting from the broad functional specifications [*untranslatable – sorry*]. It is believed that the rate of progress will continue to accelerate as necessary personnel are made available for the necessary discussions [*We will get some work done as soon as we find somebody who knows something*].

In speaking the same tendency can occur. In the example that follows, an initial statement is gradually simplified until clarity appears, as it were out of the mist. The final version is, I think, a good turn of phrase, but it is not definitive. Such a chain of improvement could doubtless continue and has in any case ultimately to reflect and suit the individual style of the speaker. You would want to say this sentence a little differently; and would feel your version was best.

Example

'Er . . . um . . . I suppose what I mean basically is what we intrinsically desire to, well, put over is sometimes not what is communicated on account of the . . . er . . . message being sort of implanted – inserted that is – in a disorganization of expression not cognizant with real – that is complete – comprehension.'

Too hesitant, too complex in words, too laborious of expression, disorganized and too long = unclear.

'What we intrinsically desire to put over is sometimes not what is communicated, on account of the messages being implanted in a disorganization of expression not cognizant with comprehension.'

Better. The meaning is beginning to be clear, but the wording is still laborious, over-complex and lacking in description = unclear.

'What we really want to say is sometimes not really clear because the true message is hidden amongst too much that is superfluous and cannot therefore be transferred to the audience.'

Better still. The meaning is surely clear but it is still awkward and lacking in description = think again.

'Sometimes the clarity we seek to convey is obscured, hidden like a diamond amongst ice. If so, an audience cannot appreciate the intended meaning of the message.'

Right. I think this is clear. I like the way it sounds (though next time I might well put it differently and feel it was improved). It is also the most succinct.

Note: in passing, another comment may be made here regarding punctuation. The *er* and *um* and *sort of* in the first part of the example act as punctuation. The next versions are lengthy and might be considered to need more punctuation. The last is simply stated and punctuated and as a result can be spoken fluently. *A good speaker is conscious of the punctuation inherent in what is delivered, and this makes for a good pace and correct emphasis.*

Figure 7.

> ### Getting your tongue round it
>
> Even assuming you do not speak too fast, it is a common fault to speak less than clearly. In a presentation, while you must speak naturally, you need to exaggerate the articulation to produce clarity and allow expression – which can never come over as well as you want if you are simply indistinct. You may find it useful to practise intentionally awkward phrases (in private by all means). Try repeating some of the following traditional tongue-twisters and sentences containing similar sounding words:
>
> - Red leather, yellow leather
> - She says she shall sew a sheet
> - She sells seashells by the sea shore
> - We're your well-wishers
>
> and, my favourite:
>
> - I'm not a pheasant plucker, I'm a pheasant plucker's son, and I'll go on plucking pheasants till the pheasant plucking's done
>
> Also:
>
> - His story is now history
> - Get some nice ice, not some nice mice
> - He hears his hiss
>
> You may have others you know and can try. Some combinations are so apt to tie the tongue they are best avoided, and this too is something it is useful to watch out for in preparation.

- *Emphasis*: this might be described as the verbal equivalent of **bold** type.

It is especially important in two ways:

- to ensure that the main points shine through, and that differing elements of a presentation (main points, examples, asides and explanation, say) are clear and stand out from the whole
- to inject animation and make what is said more interesting.

Try it

You can demonstrate the power of emphasis to yourself very easily, and experiment with it. For example, select a word or phrase the meaning of which can be changed just by saying it with a different emphasis. If you take one simple word: 'No'. It can be said in a way that is:

- definite
- *very* definite
- clearly is undecided
- might mean maybe

and more.

With a phrase it may be where in it the emphasis is put that makes the difference:

- 'I am quite *sure*'
- '*I* am quite sure'
- 'I *am* quite sure'.

Select a few and practise (again try using a tape recorder if you really want to hear the difference you can create).

All these different factors must be orchestrated together. This may sound complex, but again the initial task is to develop some good habits and, above all, to remain conscious of the possibilities. The way you use your voice can potentially add so much to the way you present.

Next consider something at the other end of the body from where the voice emanates.

Footwork

Superficially the feet may seem to have little to do with presentation. Not so; feet, and the stance that goes with them, are both important elements in the way a speaker both feels and thus comes over. Here therefore are some guidelines to help ensure comfort and assist in making a good impression. Note that footwork takes us into total posture and movement; other aspects of this are dealt with under the next heading (*Arms and hands*).

Though it may be true that people in the audience rarely look at a presenter's feet, if you make mistakes in the way you stand they will notice both the feet and the results. The first question to be investigated is therefore 'to move or not to move'. The extremes can both cause problems:

- *Too much movement*:
  - can make the speaker appear nervous
  - may channel energy away from more important areas
  - may become a distraction, of itself
  - could put you in the wrong place at the wrong time (out of reach of the projector or your notes).

- *Too little movement*:
  - can look uncomfortable
  - can become uncomfortable (you easily get stiff)
  - restricts the use of gestures and makes for a static approach.

Circumstances affect cases. You cannot move so much standing behind a lectern as you can working from behind a table for instance. Otherwise you need to find an 'ideal' that will both suit you and seem appropriate to the audience. Examples of the principles such an ideal might include follow:

- stand up straight (slouching looks slovenly – the best way of avoiding this is to imagine a string attached to the middle of the top of the head pulling straight upwards)
- keep your feet just a little apart (shoulder width – to maintain an easy balance)
- move just a little to avoid cramp and add some variety.

- move purposively (making it clear, for example, that you are moving to be near equipment or to address a questioner more directly).

Overall a relaxed, comfortable and yet professional stance will communicate confidence (perhaps beyond the level that is felt). The most suitable stance may vary depending on both the nature and duration of the event. For example, some meetings are more formal than others, some are more participative (a speaker may need to walk into the open space of a U-shaped conference layout to address people more individually), and some are simply longer (a trainer working with a group all day might acceptably lean against the table at the front, whereas a fifteen-minute presentation from a lectern may need greater formality and less variety).

> **Try it**
>
> It is practically impossible to try out stances in isolation – have a go if you like – without becoming self-conscious and stilted. But do think positively about the practicalities of this as you face individual presentational situations, and do not run before you can walk. By which I mean you may for instance create considerable rapport and emphasis by walking into the centre of a U-shaped meeting layout to deal with or make a particular point, but this will fall flat if you have to race back to your notes in mid-sentence to see what comes next.

With feet firmly on the floor we can turn to the other aspects which make up the totality of stance and posture.

Arms and hands

Both arms and hands are very much more visible and noticeable to the audience than feet, what is more they give rise to one of the most asked questions from presenters: 'What do I do with my hands?' Awkwardness about what to do with them can be a distraction to the speaker. And if they *are* awkward then they become a distraction to the audience. They should be an asset to the speaker and make a positive impression on the members of the audience. They will act in this way if gestures made are appropriate and naturally executed. Some immediate examples of use and effect illustrate their importance:

- too static a pose is awkward and distracting (and may look too formal or imply nerves)
- some static positions look protective (implying fear of the audience) e.g. arms folded or clasped in front of the body
- too much arm waving seems nervous and is equated with fidgeting (this is especially so of arm waving and hand gestures that do not seem to relate to what is being said – the Magnus Pyke school of presentation)

Conversely:

- a comfortable 'resting' position for hands and arms is comfortable for speaker and audience alike
- appropriate gestures and animation add interest, enthusiasm and emphasis. They give an impression of confidence and thus expertise.

Two key elements here are worth an individual word.

Resting

The most obvious natural position is simply standing with both hands hanging loosely by the sides. The problem here is that many people find that the more they think about it the harder it is to be natural. The only route is thus to think about it first, to decide on a number of positions that can be adopted as bases from which a period of greater animation can commence; then forget about it. Remember that, for men, in a business suit, one hand in a pocket may have an appropriate appearance; two never does, it just looks slovenly. One useful alternative to arms by the sides is to give your hands something specific and appropriate *to do*, for example:

- hold some item (perhaps a pen)
- hold onto something (perhaps a corner of a lectern or the OHP) – one hand is best here, using two can make it look as if you are hanging on for protection, so, even with one hand, avoid white knuckles!

This is certainly an area which can benefit from some thought; however, what works best is a fluid transition between these things. A natural pose, shifting to another, then into a gesture and back again. Rest assured it comes with practice and avoid becoming hyper-conscious of it. If you relax and forget you will adopt a natural pose and manner which will look right.

Gestures

These should not be overdone, but should be useful and relate to the words being used. Above all there must be some, to have no animation in this department always displays a lack-lustre impression. What can you do? Here are some examples:

- a simple directional pointing – to a slide, a member of the group, or more intangibly (a point into space as the speaker introduces 'the market and our customers')
- a fist on the table – 'NO!'
- a width gesture (like the fisherman's 'one that got away') to indicate size – 'enormous potential'
- counting on the fingers – 'First, we need . . . second, . . .' (be careful not to lose count! – people notice)
- holding up and showing an item – 'This brochure will . . .'
- a dramatic gesture – tearing up a sheet of paper.

You can no doubt think of more and must search for ones that you find comfortable to use, that will become a natural part of your approach. It is an idea, at least until confidence builds, to use a mark in your notes to prompt key gestures.

Here again we are seeing something that is dependent, at least in part, on acquiring habits. Do not worry about it too much and it will become natural, though knowing what you are aiming at will help.

> **Try it**
>
> This can be another area where practice in isolation may be so artificial as to help little. Two things are worthwhile:
>
> - Make a point of demonstrating to yourself just how much of a message comes over via the gestures. Next time you watch something on the television where someone is making a speech, turn the sound down and watch the visual alone. A few moments even will make the point.
> - Actively build in certain key gestures, as was suggested with a prompt in your notes, so that you do not fail to include them, but do not worry too much about what happens in between. You will find with practice that you begin to link them up and a more fluid pattern is built into your overall manner.

At this point we turn to something rather different. You might imagine that you are in full flood, using the principles of structure and delivery so far discussed. Everything is going really well, to your surprise your nerves have retreated into the background and then, suddenly . . . *crash, someone who has crept into the back of the room with a tray of cups drops the lot. All heads turn* . . .

Unexpected accidents

With the best will in the world (even assuming adequate preparation) not everything is going to go right every time. Sometimes there will be unexpected accidents and these can:

- throw the speaker off their stride
- disrupt the attention of the audience

or both, bearing in mind that it is mostly fear of the second that causes people to allow the first to occur. You may not know exactly what is going to happen, but you can consider in advance how to best deal with the unexpected.

First adopt the right attitude:

- accept that accidents do, occasionally, happen
- they do disrupt attention and cannot be ignored
- forewarned is forearmed.

All sorts of things can happen, elsewhere in the room as above, or it may be you who causes the accident. You spill a jug of water or put up the next slide and it is not the next slide. Reactions can vary and include reduced credibility, laughter, distraction, even pity. What is needed is a systematic response, a way of dealing with things that you drop into almost automatically, matching the specifics of what you do to the circumstances. The following provides such a basis for action:

1 Acknowledge it (it is no good pretending something has not happened). This can range from 'Oh dear' to something more humorous: 'I'll have to pay for that' if something is broken, for example

Not least this *gives you a moment to think* as you:

2 Consider the options which may range from a further remark or two while you sort something out to taking an impromptu break while the situation is recovered
3 Take the chosen action – quickly and quietly *and calmly* (remember the old saying: more haste less speed)
4 Communicate – simply tell people what is happening (this may take no longer than the action itself)
5 Restart with some punch, rather as if starting a new point.

Remember that the audience are on your side when disaster strikes. The most usual thought to flash through the mind of members of the group is: 'Thank goodness it isn't me having to deal with that!' So if something happens that could not have been avoided, then a smooth recovery is itself impressive and builds the perception of competence you no doubt want to project.

Certain things can be planned for pretty specifically. For example, if you use an overhead projector – there are few organizations that do not have one these days – what happens if the bulb blows? Does the machine have a facility simply to switch over to a second bulb? If so, then a simple acknowledgement of what you are doing and flicking a switch sorts the problem. If not, can you carry on without the projector (or is an impromptu break while the bulb is changed possible)? The answer may depend on the nature of the presentation, but having options in mind will make it easier to cope with.

Something else you can have ready is a supply of 'filler' remarks, such as the phrase: 'I'll have to pay for that' mentioned earlier. Think about what suits you and store them away; you will inevitably need something like it eventually.

So, the response to accidents should not be all doom and gloom, they may present a chance to shine. Out-and-out accidents are not the only thing you will have to cope with and another category of occurrence is worth a separate word.

Unforeseen incidents

There is certainly an overlap here, but the heading implies a different kind of event. Thus a different kind of response may be called for when there is an *accident*: these are often the speaker's fault (e.g. dropping something) or the cause is far removed from the group (e.g. a fire alarm rings in a hotel meeting room) as opposed to what is defined here as an *incident* where others may be involved.

An example will make the point. For instance, imagine that a speaker is proceeding well, let us say presenting a plan to the Board of Directors, when the meeting room door opens and a secretary or assistant enters with a tray of tea. What should the speaker do? Maybe:

- the speaker should continue
- the noise (of cups and saucers being laid out) will be a distraction
- the group is senior (the Board) it would be impolite to stop or complain
- they may have organized it this way
- it may be a mistake, the meeting should have been left undisturbed.

There is, I believe, an important rule here: *never compete with an interruption*. This means that the first response to such an incident should be to acknowledge it. The *intention* must be to:

- ensure it is clear you are not unaware of the problem (someone may well be wondering what is the matter with a speaker who carries on as if no one is distracted)
- either minimize or eliminate the interruption
- summon assistance if appropriate
- maintain as far as possible the smooth flow of the presentation
- reinforce the capability of the speaker (recovering well even from minor mishaps is often well regarded, especially by those who judge they would not have done so well).

Consider these issues further by reference to an example. For instance, consider what options the tea delivery mentioned above might pose:

- simply acknowledging it may remove it ('Perhaps the serving of the tea could wait just a few minutes until we are finished' – whoever is doing the delivery may, hearing this, beat a hasty retreat. In some groups a moment's silence might well have the same effect)
- asking the Chair (if there is one) for a view ('Would you like me to pause for a moment while the tea is laid out?' – this may prompt a number of useful responses: from agreement that you should do so, to an instruction that the tea should wait)
- adjust your timing so that you can break earlier than planned ('I see the tea is here. Let's break here therefore and I will pick up the point . . .')

Remember that it may well be necessary to complete the sentence or the point being made immediately before the event prior to interrupting to take action as above.

Both these kinds of thing, accidents and incidents, are exceptions. Do not fret about the possibility throughout a talk, but bear in mind that successful recovery makes a good impression and that forewarned is forearmed.

Three further topics need addressing before this chapter of

> **Try it**
>
> Certainly you should think about such things in advance and have a few thoughts in mind. In rehearsing a talk you might decide on a particular possible interruption and incorporate dealing with it into your practice. One colleague of mine tells me he has done this using an electric kitchen timer. He gives it a turn – without looking accurately at the time it is set for – and then regards the ensuing buzz as an interruption and practises recovering from it.

varied topics is finished. These are timing, what I call 'flourishes' and, finally, the use of humour.

Timing

In virtually all kinds of presentation, timing, in the sense of time-keeping is important. Like punctuality, which acts in part as a courtesy and saves wasting time, especially other people's time, good time-keeping shows respect for the group. You may promise little else to keep your options open, but keeping to time should be one promise which is fulfilled.

In certain circumstances, making a competitive presentation as a potential supplier for instance, time-keeping is one of a number of factors that will be taken as indicative of your attitude to service. If the prospect gives you half an hour, then you sit down after twenty-eight minutes. If you run over, you immediately lose part of their attention as they think to themselves 'How much longer than the set time is this going to take?' Worse still, they may regard it as a discourtesy, incompetence or a sign that you will care similarly little for the future service they require if they give you the business. Suddenly one of your competitors begins to look more suitable.

So, having established that it is important how do you keep to time? The following summarizes some factors that help, and in some cases pulls together points made earlier:

- use your notes to judge time, knowing how long a page in your particular style represents (you also can flag particular points: half way, at what time you should start to summarize)
- rehearse and time it, particularly where timing is key
- keep an eye on the time (with your watch on the table in front of you)
- have some options in your material, elements that can be added or dropped to match the time you are in effect taking
- take note of how long your talks take, if you aim at twenty minutes and run to only fifteen or to twenty-five, make a note of why and learn from the experience
- allow for contingency, think about how much of the time will go on the introduction from the Chair, the coffee break or questions and so on
- ask a colleague to give you a visual reminder at some pre-agreed point or time.

All these may help. Again do not despair; it does get easier to judge with practice and while you will not always get it exactly right, if you work at it you will have a reasonable chance of coming close.

As a final thought here the discipline of good time-keeping by the speaker sets an example. It is little use chastising people for returning late after coffee, or failing to be ready to start on time, if they know your own attempts at time-keeping are a joke.

A flourish

The next heading in this chapter refers to something which both shows how a number of the techniques discussed here can usefully work together to enhance their effect, and adds an extra dimension. Let me explain with some examples:

- one kind of flourish (difficult to exemplify on the page without hearing it) is simply when at a key point the emphasis and meaning are exactly and very apparently right. Rather as the punch line of a good funny story must be just right, so a phrase, a summary or key point comes over to perfection. This may involve finding just the right turn of phrase, delivering it with just the right emphasis and timing and with a matching gesture that suits the moment, and carrying it out with apparent natural ease. It is, if you like, a peak of the animation that needs to constantly enliven any address. As such it is an exceptional moment. The whole talk cannot be like this, though some need, by their nature, more of it than others. Sometimes a particular passage simply lends itself to this and inspiration fires it up as it is delivered. On other occasions the effect is well planned; sometimes too, it combines a little of both.

- another kind of flourish involves an appropriate (again usually but not always thought-out) 'event' that is added specifically to enliven. For example, I was once in the audience at a meeting where one speaker made a dramatic start: 'Ladies and Gentlemen,' he began, 'I know time is short and I will take no more than my allotted hour to . . .'. The Chairman, who sat beside him, looked horrified, tugged his sleeve and pointed to his watch. The speaker glanced in his direction for a second, and continued: 'Of course, I am so sorry,' he said. 'It is half an hour.' As he said this he lifted his notes and tore them in half lengthways down the page, thus apparently halving the duration of his talk. He then restarted. Already the group were giving him their complete attention.
- on another occasion I saw someone involve a member of the group he was addressing to create such a flourish. He was setting out some changes in policy affecting budgets. There were cutbacks and much carping about certain expenses, as someone had said: 'only a fiver', no longer being allowed. He asked if anyone had a five pound note. Someone handed one over. He promptly tore it up, sprinkling the pieces across the table to the clear horror of the volunteer. 'But it's *only a fiver*' he said going on to contrast the attitude of many people towards what they see as 'company' money or 'my' money. It made a dramatic point (though it cost him a fiver! – he had to repay the money later).

Such actions need an element of creativity, but you can plan their inclusion in what you do. There are, of course, dangers here. There is nothing worse than a dramatic gesture that falls flat so you need to progress with some care. The combining of a number of factors, both verbal and physical, to create particular impact is something that adds to the overall impression a presentation makes. When done well it is seamless. In other words, the whole presentation flows smoothly along, there is variety of pace and emphasis and an occasional flourish is reached smoothly and naturally as a high point in the presentation's progress. The intention is for the emphasis achieved to be more striking than the method of achieving it.

A flourish may include another factor as yet unmentioned, that of humour.

A funny thing . . .

Humour is invaluable for varying the pace, changing the mood, providing an interval and – perhaps more important – reinforcing a point. But . . . humour is a funny business, and needs sensitive handling. It should not be overdone; it was Noel Coward who said: 'Wit ought to be a glorious treat, like caviar; never spread it around like marmalade.' This last sentence is designed to illustrate just how humour can work in a presentation. It does not have to make people roll around laughing (the quote above is mildly amusing but cleverly put). It certainly provides a light moment, but it makes a point too with what it says. Most business presentations are not appropriate to a great deal of hilarity, but many can usefully include a smile or two. And some may have a more social connotation and need more, as with say a retirement party: 'I well remember the day John started work here. I overheard two girls in the Accounts office talking about him. One said: "Doesn't that Mr Green dress well" and the other replied, "Yes, and so quickly".'

Humour is, however, difficult to judge. What one group may laugh out loud at raises not a murmur from another, and there is nothing so flat as an out-and-out joke that falls flat. Back to Noel Coward, because a quotation has some safety built in, particularly if it contains clear content or a moral. People may only smile inwardly for a moment but it lifts the proceedings and varies the pace, perhaps also having a positive effect on the rapport being established between the speaker and the audience. If you want to be sure of raising a serious smile then the humour must be tested, something you know from past experience works. It is more important for it to be successful, and pertinent, than for it to be original.

Short, witty injections, of which quotes are but one example, work better in many circumstances than long stories. If a longer story does not work, or even does not work particularly well, then it can act to dilute the effectiveness of what is being done. Because of this it is usually better to include any humour as an aside rather than as a big production number, if it does not work very well then no matter, you can quickly move on. If it has a moral, then that may make a mark without proving very humorous, and this may still be fine.

The link to the topic is important. Examples in print are not the same as something delivered in the right way 'on the day'; however, let me risk an example of the smile rather than belly-laugh variety. Another quote: the late Isaac Asimov, the well-known and prolific science fiction writer, was once asked what he would do if he heard he only had six months to live. He replied in two words: 'Type faster'. I quoted this recently on a seminar I was conducting on business writing skills and it certainly raised a smile. More important it linked well to the topic and there are, in context, a variety of ways it can then be linked to the time it takes to get, say, a report right, or to the productivity factor inherent in such work. Something so brief is doubly useful. It does not disrupt the flow or take over the proceedings, and can be glossed over if you pick something that works less well than you would like. Some commend the idea of having back-up comments to use noted in your running guide. If the first falls a little flat you can rapidly add a further, better, comment, though beware of digging the hole deeper if *neither* works well.

Again this is not an area on which to overstretch yourself. If the only appropriate story you can think of needs an accurate foreign accent to make it work, omit it if the accent is outside your repertoire. If timing is not your forte or if you cannot remember the punch line, avoid anything complex or work from an especially clear note. Some stories or quips have an awkwardness about them in terms of delivery. For example, one business quip I like is of the man who discovered the perfect business plan to make real profit: he purchased MBAs for what they were worth, and sold them for what they *thought* they were worth. Nothing elaborate and it will not engender more than a quiet smile, but you have to get it the right way round. What is seemingly simple in print can become ridiculously tongue-tying on your feet at a key moment in your presentation – this is just the sort of thing to ensure is completely clear in any note you have in front of you.

Despite the *caveats* stated here, humour is an important element of many a presentation. It can act to break the ice early on, to change the mood, to provide a memorable image to assist retention of the message, and can contain a moral or truth that is very much part of the message. In addition you may want to have a quip or two up your sleeve for use as 'fillers' or in response to incidents, for example greeting an interrupting telephone ring with: 'I keep telling her not to ring me at work', before making a more practical comment to deal with it. I keep meaning to record more systematically than I do stories I have heard or found useful. I know some people who do so and are never stuck for an appropriate tale. Appropriate includes the vexed question of good taste. Horses for courses, but in public it is usually best to keep off anything sensitive, such as religion or politics, you only have to upset one member of a group to sound a sour note. Keep in mind the nature of the group, what you know about them and work from that.

If you do not want to be seen as delivering verbal Mogadon you will need to use some humour at least occasionally. As an example, and to provide a light-hearted end to this chapter, let me quote one story I stole and used on a company conference to lead in to the serious matter of financial resources:

> A smart, new, top-of-the-range Volvo estate, boot full of expensive riding gear, tow bar, driven by a very smart rather 'county', and clearly well-off lady is attempting – very inexpertly – to park in the last space in the car park. As it backs up to try again for the twenty-seventh time, a flashy sporting

saloon of the kind that comes with built-in bumptiousness and with a driver to match, nips through the gap into the space.

The driver gets out and, as he locks the door, shouts to the Volvo driver: 'That's what you can do if you can drive properly.' The Volvo is put promptly into reverse and driven back hard into the side of the sports car, the tow bar digging deeply into the door. In the silence after the sickening crash the lady winds down the window and calls over: 'And that, young man, is what you can do if you have money!'

The old ones are often best! But it remains an area to plan with some care, I always remember a rhyme about after-dinner speaking said by the humorist Dennis Norden:

> I am gentle by nature, not stormy
> But a dam inside of me broke
> When the man who was speaking before me
> Wound up with my opening joke.

6 Making it Visual

> Seeing is believing
> *Proverb*

Everyone knows the saying that a picture is worth a thousand words. There is a great deal of truth in it. One aspect of the psychology of how people take in information is simply that seeing as well as hearing makes it more likely that attention will be maintained and that information gained as a result will be retained. There are a variety of ways of accommodating this principle in a presentation. These range from the body language of manner and gesture to which reference has already been made, to exhibits, checklist and the now ubiquitous overhead projector slide.

Visual aids are not always necessary or appropriate, but they often are both and can add an extra dimension to an otherwise routine presentation. As such they are important. For the audience they represent a proven aid to maintaining interest in a variety of ways. For the speaker they can act as an additional prompt and guide (supplementing or even replacing notes) to the sequence of points they wish to make – for example, if you are using overhead projector slides, say, the next one waiting to be shown, and visible only to you, acts as a reminder and prompt to what is next on the agenda. In addition, framed overhead projector slides can have additional notes written on the frame to guide the speaker while remaining invisible to the members of the group.

One key premise should be noted before any detailed consideration of visual aids. That is that visuals should *support* the presentation, not lead it. Sometimes the sheer quantity or nature of the visuals ends up overpowering, even distracting from, the speaker and the tail ends up wagging the dog.

Two extreme examples of this appear in the boxed paragraph that follows.

Two cases of 'sliditis'

The two cases here make the point about the dangers of letting the slides take over to the point where they blind the presenter to the needs of the audience:

(i) In one City firm client presentations had not been their habit. They were becoming more and more important, but many members of the team were apprehensive about them and worried about the time it took to prepare them.

What they did have were a very expensively produced set of 35mm slides about what they called 'the background to the firm' – its history, development and internal organization. The set consisted of a couple of dozen slides. The trouble was that they became a crutch. People used them – all of them – without any deep thought about how relevant they were to a particular audience. They knew them, they were comfortable with them – what better way to start a presentation?

Audiences lost out in two ways. Too much background, presented on automatic pilot, then a change of pace, sometimes for the worse, as the next session was slotted onto the lengthy introduction and more hesitatingly presented. The habits that were encouraged by this approach were somewhat introspective – just when the prime focus should have been on the group.

(ii) Another firm were in the design business. Their business was very visual and they rightly used many visual images in presenting to clients and prospects. The first job was to select what to show to demonstrate their expertise in a way that linked tightly to a particular prospect need, then to embed this aspect appropriately within a tailored presentation majoring on the individual circumstances of the case.

The slides began not to support but to lead. Questions about the relevance rather than the excellence were asked less thoroughly, until one day they were asked to tender for an important job with a major national charity. There were meetings, proposals and more meetings, and finally they were successfully short-listed with one other prospective supplier and asked to present to the full governing committee of the charity.

They burnt the midnight oil, planned and prepared and, of course, they assembled the slides – thirty-six of them (representing no small cost). The day of the presentation came, the three executives involved took a taxi to the office where it was to be held and were shown to the committee room. They asked, projector in hand, where the power point was located. Puzzled looks and talk of slides produced more puzzled looks, indeed mounting horror on the face of the secretary who had shown them upstairs.

The reason? They were in the headquarters of a major charity for the blind. 'You do realize eighty per cent of the committee members are blind,' said the puzzled secretary. They put the slides away and two minutes later they began to struggle through the presentation without them. It did not go very well, and they did not get the work. Honestly: *no one had thought of it*. They were bright people but stuck on the tramlines of *'how we do presentations'*. It can – and did – happen; enough to make anyone take on a more open-minded and audience-focused attitude to preparation.

Let us be clear, visuals are there to do a number of things including:

- reinforce
- exemplify
- illustrate
- explain (as a graph does with figures)

and add variety to the overall presentation and all it includes.

Too many visuals of any sort can overpower the presentation or make it seem mechanistic as every thought or new point is routinely accompanied by a new slide. Too much activity to sort and show them distracts (especially if the speaker appears unfamiliar or inexpert at what needs to be done).

Overall, they are valuable, however and in summary can:

- present a great deal of information quickly
- improve the understanding of a presentation
- give visible structure to the verbal communication
- *allow a visualization* of the main thrust of an argument, and 'position' the message before it is examined in detail.

It is worth considering the nature of visualization here for a moment. Some things are difficult, if not impossible, to describe in words. How well can you describe, for example, how the knot on a man's necktie is tied? – without any hand gestures! Not easy. Certain things are clearly prime candidates for visualization, for example:

- figures: a graph, bar or pie chart can present information at a glance that most of us would take some time to discern from a mass of figures (see figure 8 below)

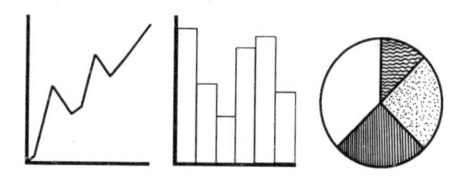

Figure 8. *Information presented on a) a graph b) a bar chart c) a pie chart*

- humour (amongst other things) can be put over in cartoon form
- diagrams, such as a flow chart, present a complex situation almost literally as a picture
- a link can be made between a picture and a concept or abstract thought, for example in figure 9 below (in fact the cover illustration for my Sheldon Press book *How to Negotiate Successfully*) a visual image well illustrates the concept of the many 'variables of negotiation' being weighed up.

Figure 9. *The negotiation variables 'weighed up'*

Of course, many business slides consist primarily of words. These are rather different in nature and act as signposts and checklists to keep what may be a complex and building argument on track. Turning to the method, the most common forms of visual aid are:

- flip charts
- overhead projectors or viewgraphs
- table-top presenters
- fixed whiteboards
- handouts.

The advantages of such visual displays can be compared as follows:

Flip charts

Advantages	Disadvantages
• no power source needed	• expensive to prepare professionally
• can be prepared beforehand	• very large and cumbersome to carry to an outside venue
• can be adapted on the spot	
• easy to see	• masking is difficult and can be untidy
• usually available in some form	
• easy to write on	• can sometimes look messy
• colour can be used	• may not stand up to constant use.
• you can refer back to earlier sheets.	

In general, flip charts are more useful as a group 'work pad' than as the basis of a presentation.

Overhead projectors

Advantages	Disadvantages
• can be seen in even a bright room	• need a power source
	• can be noisy

- produce a large image
- masking (obscuring the bottom part of a slide and revealing it progressively) is easily possible
- prepared slides easily carried
- can look professional
- commonly available
- can be used sitting down
- *aide-memoire* notes can be written on slide frame

- projection lens can block the view of the screen
- can break down
- limit to amount of information that can be legibly projected
- require a screen or a suitable wall
- tidy use requires discipline and experience

With acetate roll attached:

- can also be used as a group workpad.

- not easy to write on without practice
- overhead projectors providing an acetate roll facility are usually bulky machines, though modern 'flat' overhead projectors are available with an acetate roll built in.

Overhead projectors are generally best used as the prepared base of a presentation, while the acetate roll is more useful as a 'work pad'. (see page 97)

Table-top presenters ('mini-flip charts')

Advantages
- all the advantages of a flipchart
- easier to prepare professionally
- easily carried and 'put up' in a training room
- can be used when seated
- more informal, yet professional.

Disadvantages
- can look too 'flashy' to some groups
- masking is not easy
- require skill to ensure they remain only an *aid*
- only work with small numbers.

Generally, table-top presenters are an effective compromise, allowing pages to be prepared in advance and 'work-pad' notes to be made. They also facilitate alterations.

Fixed white boards

Advantages	Disadvantages
• increasingly available in training rooms, etc.	• need special pens
• useful for 'work-pad' noting to aid group discussion	• not easy to write on
	• limited space
• often metal-backed, allowing prepared papers to be displayed with magnetic disks.	• usually require erasing of writing before additional comments can be displayed.

Useful only as a 'work-pad' on which to highlight a few key points.

Handouts

Advantages	Disadvantages
• can portray our professionalism	• usually not personalized
• highlighting of relevant points is possible	• parts of content can be irrelevant or even counter-productive
• can convey our technical expertise and give third party references.	• can detract from our verbal presentation.

Generally useful as a support for the presentation argument, but it is not easy to condition and control the perception of the aid itself.

Increasingly, other aids – 35 mm slides, video tapes, computer displays – are entering the presentational arena. Most can be excellent in their place. Most also distance the audience from the presenter. The most successful presenters will therefore use them with caution, since they know the final impact will be dependent upon the participants' acceptance of the credibility of the speaker and the message, not on the supporting elements.

Figure 10 sets out the general principles for the preparation of visual aids and, to focus on perhaps the most used and most useful, figure 11 reviews in detail how to use an OHP effectively.

Figure 10. *General principles of preparing visual aids*

- Keep the content simple
- Restrict the number of words:
  - use single words to give structure, headings, or short statements
  - do not cause the aid to look cluttered and complicated
  - personalize with firm's name or logo where possible (or the talk's title)
- Use diagrams, graphs, etc., where possible to present figures. Never read figures alone without visual support
- Build in a variety within the overall common theme:
  - use colour
  - build in variations of the forms of aids used
- Emphasize the theme and the structure:
  - continually use one of the aids as the recurring reminder of the objective and agenda (e.g. prepared flip chart)
  - make logical use of the aids (e.g. overhead projector for base of presentation, flip chart or whiteboard for highlighting comment)
- Ensure the content of the visual matches the words:
  - make the content relevant
- Ensure the visuals can be seen:
  - are they clear?
  - what are the room limitations?
  - what are the equipment limitations?
  - use strong colour
  - beware of normal type-face reproduced on slides unless enlarged
- Ensure the layout emphasizes the meaning the aid should convey.

Figure 11. *Using an overhead projector*

Some care should be taken in using overhead projectors to begin with; they appear deceptively simple, but present inherent hazards to the unwary. The following hints may be useful:

- make sure the electric flex is out of the way (or taped to the floor); falling over it will improve neither presentation nor dignity.
- make sure you have a spare bulb (and know how to change it) – though many machines contain a spare you can switch over to automatically – test both.
- make sure it is positioned as you want; for example, on a stand or a table on which there is room for notes, etc. Left-handed people will want it placed differently from right-handed people.
- stand back and to the side of it; it is easy to obscure the view of the screen.
- having made sure that the picture is in focus, look primarily at the machine and not at the screen; the machine's prime advantage is to keep you facing the front.
- only use slides that have big enough typefaces or images and, if you plan to write on acetate, check that the size of your handwriting is appropriate.
- switch off while changing slides, otherwise the group see a jumbled image as one is removed and replaced by another.
- if you want to project the image on a slide progressively you can cover the bottom part of the image with a sheet of paper (use paper that is not too thick and you will be able to see the image through it, although the covered portion will not project).
- for handwritten use, an acetate roll, rather than sheets, fitted running from the back of the machine to the front will minimize the amount of acetate used (it is expensive!).
- remember that when something new is shown, all attention goes, at least momentarily, to the slide; as concentration on what you are saying will be less, stop talking until this moment has passed.
- it may be useful to add emphasis by highlighting certain things on slides as you go through them; if you slip the slide *under* a sheet or roll of acetate you can do so without marking the slide.
- similarly, two slides shown together can add information (this may be done with overlays attached to the slide and folded across); alternatively, the second slide may have minimal information on it, with such things as a course title, session heading or company logo remaining in view through the whole, or part of, the session. Alternatively, masters can be used to provide various standard backgrounds to which other words or images can be added.

If you want to point something out, this is most easily done by laying a small pointer (or pencil) on the projector. Extending pointers are (in my view) almost impossible to use without looking pretentious, and they risk you having to look over your shoulder.

Finally, in what is an important area, the main rules in using visual aids are:

- Talk to the group, not the visuals.
- Use colour to highlight key points.
- Talk to the group while writing on a visual aid.
- Avoid impeding the group's view of visual aids.
- Explain graphs and figures or any complex chart.
- Remove an aid immediately when it is no longer required.
- Tell the participants what they will receive as copies. It is often useful to issue slides in hard copy after the session.

Anything else?

Remember that anything – virtually anything – may be used as a visual aid. An exhibit, something held aloft to make a point, may be just as effective (more so on occasions) than a more conventional visual aid. Some examples I have seen or used over the years make the point:

- an onion (to make a point about market segmentation)
- maps
- money (to link to financial content)
- newspapers/magazines (a quote – something topical perhaps – read out is one thing, read out of the actual original publication is another)
- product (whatever your company makes, if this is appropriate)
- people (from a waiter in a hotel to a girl in a bikini, to make points about customer service and, as I remember, visual aids!)
- models (of products too large to use themselves)
- a watch or clock (to make a point about time-keeping).

> **Try it**
>
> While this thought is in your mind write down any ideas it brings to mind for the situations you face – do not let a good idea escape for want of making a note.

Finally in this chapter a word about the equipment visual aids demand.

Check, check and check again

The message here is very simple: *always check all the equipment before your talk begins*. All of it. Not just that the overhead projector lights up (and that slides are legible at the back of the room), but that the slides fit, are in focus, and that the acetate roll, if there is one, goes round. And that you are not going to trip over the wire, that you can locate the switch easily and . . . but you get the point.

As an example of what not checking can do from one well-remembered incident, a company put on an important customer presentation at a hotel. One segment of it used 35mm slides for which the room was blacked out. As several members of staff were involved the last speaker handed over to his successor, dimmed the lights and left the room. While the slides were shown, the evening darkened (it was a winter afternoon) and when the projector was finally switched off the room was really totally dark. No one present knew where the light switches were. Ten minutes of fumbling eventually found the telephone and someone from the hotel came and showed them the switches in a cupboard in the wall, at which point the original speaker reappeared wanting to know what all the fuss was about.

For many months afterwards customers talked about 'that presentation in the dark' and a public relations exercise was much diluted in its effect. Such is the fragility of such occasions.

To digress slightly, for the detail of more complex equipment is beyond our brief (whether it is back projection or a computer screen linked to a projector, the moral is the same: never let the technical people go until you are 110 per cent sure everything is working and you can continue unaided), one item most presenters come across once in a while is the microphone. Briefly, the key rules about them are:

- *always try them in advance*: it is important to judge the volume at which you speak and this may take a moment to adjust to and this, in turn, may be distracting to both speaker and audience if it is done in the first moments of a talk
- microphones *which move*, for instance the kind that clip to your lapel, are much easier for the inexperienced as you do not constantly have to remember to keep the right distance from them
- if speaking with a *fixed microphone* make sure you find a way of keeping your distance constant (e.g. at a lectern a hand on it to measure the distance away you stand is helpful)
- with fixed microphones you should *avoid* violent movement and doing things that are noisy (e.g. things like the rustle of paper are exaggerated over a sound system).

At this point we next turn again to the continuing reason for everything so far reviewed; the audience.

7 Involvement

> The best audience is intelligent,
> well educated and a little drunk
> *Alben W Barkley*

Audiences are important as has been stressed throughout, but they are not simply a passive target. They may sometimes be involved. Certainly there should always be a link with them. Eye contact has been mentioned in the last chapter. So too the feedback that comes from it and from general observation of the sounds and signs of the group and from individual members of it.

In small groups presentations may sometimes be only a step removed from a round table meeting. A manager at the head of a boardroom table may be on his feet and presenting, yet still engage individual members of the group in individual exchanges – to obtain more pointed and immediate feedback perhaps: 'What is your view of this Mary?' Too far in this direction takes us into training or perhaps counselling (there is thus some overlap here with my book *Running an Effective Training Session* [Gower Publishing]. Here, in the context of formal presentations, involvement is taken to mean the process of encouraging – where necessary or desirable – and dealing with questions.

So, how do we deal with this? In three stages: *when* to take questions, *how to prompt them* when desired and *how to answer them*.

When to take questions

The first thing to be said here is that the option to decide when to take questions may not be that of the speaker. If an invitation to speak is issued, then the format of the meeting may well be fixed. This is likely to be the case both internally within an organization or externally. Always find out what the format of a particular meeting is and if you think some variant would be better (either for you or for the meeting) *consider* asking whoever is in charge if the format might be adjusted. Be careful; if you demand your own way in some situations it may do you no good at all – you may be better to live with, and make the best of, the arrangements. Different situations demand different approaches, and sometimes a specific suggestion will be welcomed.

Broadly the options are:

- to take questions at any time through the presentation (this should only be done if you are able and willing to keep control as it can prove disruptive; also you must be sure you are going to cope well with the questions or an early one that gets you flustered can dent the best of starts)
- taking questions at the end of the session (though this can frustrate the audience and may give you a false sense of security if you believe everything you are saying is being completely accepted)
- a mix of both, perhaps a main question session at the end, but one or two on the way through
- no questions.

Most presentations may well be followed by questions; indeed you may wish to prompt them to create discussion or debate, or simply to avoid an embarrassing gap at the end of the session. One important point is relevant here. You will often do best to keep the last word for yourself. A danger of a question session end is that it tails away and, especially if someone else is in the Chair, the final word is taken away from you. After a few questions, they are slower coming, the last one is somewhat insubstantial perhaps and the Chair ends the meeting: 'Well, there seem to be no more questions, let's leave it there and thank . . .'

A better route can be to introduce question time in a way that reserves the right to the final word, even through the Chair: 'Right, Mr Chairman, perhaps we should see if there are any questions. Then perhaps I could reserve two minutes to summarize before we close.'

Directing questions

There are several ways of directing questions; they can be:

- *Overhead questions*: put to the group generally, and useful for opening up a subject (if there is no response, then you can move on to the next method): 'Right, what do you think the key issue here is? Anyone?'
- *Overhead and then directed at an individual*, useful to make the whole group think before looking for an answer from one person: 'Right, what do you think the key issues here are? Anyone? . . . John, what do you think?'
- *Direct to individual*, useful for obtaining individual responses, testing for understanding: 'John, what do you think . . . ?'
- *non-response/rhetorical*, useful where you want to make a point to one or more persons in the group without concentrating on anyone in particular, or for raising a question you would expect to be in the group's mind and then answering it yourself: 'What's the key issue? Well, perhaps it's . . .'

All these methods represent very controlled discussion, i.e. speaker . . . group member . . . speaker . . . another group member (or more), but . . . back to the speaker. Two other types help to open up a discussion:

- *Re-directed questions*, useful to make others in the group answer any individual's answer: 'That's a good point John. What do you think the answer is, Mary?'
- *Developmental questioning*, where you take the answer to a previous question and move it around the audience, building on it: 'Having established that, how about . . . ?'

Whichever of the above is being used, certain principles should be borne in mind. For questioning to be effective, the following general method may be a useful guide to the kind of sequence that can be employed:

- *State the question clearly and concisely*. Questions should relate directly to the subject being discussed. Whenever possible they should require people to think, to draw on their past experiences, and relate them to the present circumstances.

- *Ask the question first to the group rather than to an individual.* If the question is directed to a single individual, others are off the hook and do not have to think about the answer. Direct, individual questions are more useful to break a general silence in the group, or to involve someone who is not actively participating in the discussion.
- *After asking the question, pause.* Allow a few moments for the group to consider what the answer should be. Then . . .
- *Ask a specific individual to answer.* The four-step process starts the entire group thinking because they never know who will be called on. Thus everyone has to consider each question you ask, and be ready to participate. Even those who are not called on are still involved.

To be sure of using an effective questioning technique, there are some points which should be avoided, such as:

- *Asking yes or no questions.* Participants can attempt to guess the answer (and may be right). These questions should not be used if you want participants to use their reasoning power and actively participate.
- *Asking tricky questions.* Remember, your purpose is to inform people, not to antagonize them or make them look bad. Difficult questions, yes. Tricky, no. Keep personalities and sarcasm out of your questions.
- *Asking unanswerable questions.* You want to provide knowledge, not confusion. Be sure that the knowledge and experience of your group are such that at least some participants can answer the questions you're asking. Never attempt to highlight ignorance by asking questions which the group can't handle. And this is particularly true when you're trying to draw out a silent participant and involve them. Be sure they can answer before you ask them the questions.
- *Asking personal questions.* Personal questions are usually rather sensitive, even in one-to-one sessions. They are often inappropriate in a group session.
- *Asking leading questions.* By leading questions, we mean ones in which the speaker indicates the preferred answer in advance: 'Mary, don't you agree that this new form will help solve the

problem?' Such questions require little effort on the part of the participant, and little learning takes place. In addition, even if Mary didn't agree, she would probably be uncomfortable saying so. After all, that does not seem to be the answer you want.

- *Repeating questions.* Don't make a practice of repeating the question for an inattentive person. Doing so simply encourages further inattention and wastes valuable time. Instead, ask someone else to respond. People will quickly learn that they have to listen.
- *Allowing group answers.* Unless written down (and then referred to around the group), questions that allow several members of the group to answer are not useful. First, everyone cannot talk at once. Second, with group answers a very few participants may well tend to dominate the session. And third, group answers allow the silent person to hide and not participate as they should.

Note: the one unbreakable rule all sessions should have, clearly understood and adhered to, is ONLY ONE PERSON MAY TALK AT ONCE (and the speaker must be the acknowledged referee and decide who has the floor at any particular moment).

Above all, let your questioning be natural. Ask because you want to know – because you want this information to be shared with the group. Never think of yourself as a quizmaster with certain questions that must be asked whether or not they're timely. Let your manner convey your interest in the response you're going to get, and be sure that your interest is genuine. Forced, artificial enthusiasm will never fool a group.

Handling questions

As questions come, prompted or otherwise, you need to think about how you answer them. The following suggested approach will help.

- get the question right and never try to answer a point when you are actually not quite clear what is meant. If necessary ask for it to be repeated, check it back 'What you are asking is . . .

is that correct?') and make a written note of it if this helps. With the question clear you can proceed to:

- acknowledge the question and questioner
- ensure, as necessary, that the question is heard and understood by the rest of the group
- give short informative answers whenever possible, and link to other parts of your message, as appropriate.

If you opt, which you may want to, for questions at any time, remember it is perfectly acceptable to:

- hold them for a moment until you finish making a point
- delay them; saying you will come back to it, in context in, say, the next session. (Then you must remember. Make a note of both the point and who made it.)
- refuse them. Some may be irrelevant or likely to lead to too much of a digression, but be *careful* not to do this too often, to respect the questioner's feelings, and to explain why you are doing so
- and if you don't know the answer, you *must* say so. You can offer to find out, you can see if anyone else in the group knows, you can make a note of it for later, but if you attempt, unsuccessfully, to answer you lose credibility. No one, in fact, expects you to be omniscient, so do not worry about it: if you are well prepared it will not happen often in any case.

A final dimension here is worth additional comment. Some 'questions' (or statements) may be negative, contradictory; or both.

Handling objections

If your presentations are not contentious and are one way, then objections may well be no problem. If you actually do get objections voiced then they must be dealt with carefully. The first rule is to make sure you have the point made straight in your mind before you respond (remember the old maxim that it is best to engage the brain before the mouth). There is nothing to say you cannot answer a question with a question to clarify the query. Or repeat it back, varying the words: 'What you are asking is . . . have I got that right?' Similarly, you may want to delay an answer, and there is no reason why that cannot be made to sound perfectly acceptable: 'That's certainly something I have to explain, perhaps I can pick it up, in context, when I get to . . .'.

It is wise also not to rush into an answer. Give it a moment (and yourself time to think – you may be amazed, and relieved, how much can go on in your mind even in a pause of just two or three seconds, a gap that is not a problem to the audience who may, in any case, expect you to consider the matter). Remember also that too glib an answer may be mistrusted; and a slight pause giving the impression of consideration may be just what is needed. A pause and an acknowledgement go well together, and also extend your private thinking time. It works well especially if the acknowledgement can be positive and make it clear you are not denying the point – or at least the relevance of it. Phrases like 'That's a good point' really can be appropriate; better still, something that makes it clear that you are going to respond or explain further: 'You're right. Cost is certainly a key issue. It *is* a great deal of money, let me say a word more about why I believe it is a good investment . . .'. Remember the answer may need to make a point to the whole audience rather than only to the individual who voiced doubts.

A final – important – point here. Never be afraid to say 'I don't know'. People are unlikely to expect you to be omniscient in any case. You can offer to check a point later, you can ask if others in the group know, but the dangers of bluffing are all too apparent. You can end up having dug a very deep hole for yourself.

Audiences are not, of course, entirely homogeneous groups. All sorts of people may be present (this affects the intentions of the speaker, as has already been intimated) but it also affects the handling of questions. Different people have different attitudes, motivations and manners and may put questions in many different ways. The boxed section sets out some examples of types of questioner and tactics to deal with each. Some are all too common, others will rarely have to be dealt with, still others only occur when question sessions slip into more open discussion.

Figure 12. *Dealing with different styles of questioner*

- *The 'show-off'*
  Avoid embarrassing or shutting them off; you may need them later.
  Solution: toss him a difficult question. Or say, '*That's an interesting point. Let's see what the group thinks of it.*'
- *The 'quick reactor'*
  Can also be valuable later, but can keep others out of the discussion. Solution: thank him; suggest we put others to work.
- *The 'heckler'*
  This one argues about every point being made.
  Solution: Remain calm. Agree, affirm any good points, but toss bad points to the group for discussion. They will be quickly rejected. Privately try to find out what's bothering him, try to elicit his cooperation.
- *The 'rambler'*
  Who talks about everything except the subject under discussion.
  Solution: At a pause in his monologue, thank him, return to and restate relevant points of discussion, and go on.
- *The 'mutual enemies'*
  When there is a clash of personalities.
  Solution: Emphasize points of agreement, minimize differences. Or frankly ask that personalities be left out. Draw attention back to the point being made.
- *The 'pig-headed'*
  He absolutely refuses, perhaps through prejudice, to accept points being discussed.
  Solution: Throw his points to the group, have them straighten him out. Tell him time is short, that you'll be glad to discuss it with him later.
- *The 'digresser'*
  Who takes the discussion too far off track.
  Solution: Take the blame yourself. Say, '*Something I said must have led you off the subject; this is what we should be discussing . . .*'

- *The 'professional gripe'*
  Who makes frankly political points.
  Solution: Politely point out that we cannot change policy here; the objective is to operate as best we can under the present system. Or better still, have a member of the group answer him.
- *'The 'whisperers'*
  Who hold private conversations, which while they could be related to the subject, are distracting.
  Solution: Do not embarrass them. Direct some point to one of them by name, ask an easy question. Or repeat the last point and ask for comments.
- *The 'inarticulate'*
  Who has the ideas, but can't put them across.
  Solution: Say, '*Let me repeat that . . . (then put it in better language).*'
- *The 'mistaken'*
  Who is clearly wrong.
  Solution: Say, '*That's one way of looking at it, but how can we reconcile that with . . . (state the correct point)?*'
- *The 'silent'*
  Who could be shy, bored, indifferent, insecure, or he just might learn best by listening.
  Solution: Depends on what is causing the silence. If bored or indifferent, try asking a provocative question, one you think he might be interested in. If shy, compliment him when he *does* say something, and then ask him direct questions from time to time to draw him in.

Chairmanship

This overlaps outside the brief for this book a little; however, it is useful in the context of question sessions to refer to it briefly and this checklist below, reproduced from my *The Meetings Pocketbook* (Management Pocketbooks), reviews the whole question of conducting and participating in any type of business or committee meeting.

Checklist

Chairing/leading a meeting: guidelines for conducting the whole meeting (which might include presentation, discussion and debate, and questions).

The person directing the meeting must:

- command the respect of those attending
- do their homework and come prepared, having read any relevant documents and taken any other action necessary to help them 'take charge' (they should also encourage others to prepare, this makes for more considered and succinct contributions to the meeting and saves time)
- be punctual
- start on time
- ensure administrative matters will be taken care of correctly (e.g. refreshments, taking minutes, etc.)
- start on the right note and lead into the agenda
- introduce the people, if necessary (and certainly know who's who themselves – namecards can help at some kinds of meeting)
- set the rules
- control the discussion, and the individual types present (the talkative, the quiet, the argumentative, etc.)
- encourage contributions where necessary
- ask questions to clarify (this can be a great time saver). Always query something unclear at once. If the meeting runs on when something has been misinterpreted it will take longer to sort out and you will have to recap and re-cover a section)
- ensure everybody has their say
- keep the discussion to the point
- listen, as in LISTEN. The leader resolves any 'But you said . . .' arguments
- watch the clock, and remind people of the time pressure
- summarize, clearly and succinctly, where necessary, which usually means regularly

- ensure decisions are actually made, agreed and recorded
- cope with upsets, outbursts and emotion
- provide the final word (summary) and bring things to a conclusion (and link to any final administrative detail, things like setting another meeting date are often forgotten)
- see, afterwards, to any follow-up action (another great time-waster is people arriving at meetings not having taken action promised at a previous session)
- do all this with patience, goodwill, humour and respect for the various individuals present.

One last point to end this chapter – the way a presentation is run and how the group is handled will have a considerable influence on how a question session goes. If the presentation is lack-lustre, the audience's attention is not held, or indeed if the content – perhaps a contentious policy matter – has affected their mood then any speaker will tend to get a hard time as questions are asked frankly to make a point and catch the speaker out (and perhaps impress others). On the other hand, a speaker in control of the situation, of apparent expertise and authority, is always treated with a little more circumspection when it comes to question time. So prevention and cure is a good way of looking at this area. Do your homework, know your stuff, do not be afraid to say 'I don't know' (though not *too* often!) and you will handle the presentation and the questions successfully.

Afterword

> Desperately accustomed as
> I am to public speaking
> *Noel Coward*

'Ladies and Gentlemen – readers (and to qualify for that description you have to have read your way through to this point, not flicked a page or two in from the back) – at the end of this review of the process of presentation let me conclude by putting one or two matters in context, and looking at the future.

There are essentially two aspects to what must be done to improve presentations skills. The first, assisted I hope by reading this book, is to have a sound appreciation of the techniques and processes that make a presentation go well. They provide the foundation from which you can work and expand your capabilities. Second, you need practice. This can come from attending a course, and – if you use video – not only having a chance to see how you come over, but to discuss the detail of this with other members of the group and with the tutor. A course will also allow you quickly to see other examples of the kinds of things that have to be tackled in a variety of different presentational situations. Or, of course, you can gain experience from actually making real presentations, and the idea of seeking out opportunities to accelerate that experience was mentioned in the text.

Presentation is a skill where the process of adding usefully to your experience is, you will find, never ending. There are a number of ways in which you can continue to acquire knowledge about the techniques:

- reading additional books and other references on the topic
- seeing training films on the subject

- meeting and discussing with colleagues (especially to plan or review actual future talks or run constructive post-mortems on past ones)
- rehearsing in front of colleagues and noting comments before going on to a final version (supervising rehearsals is something I am regularly asked to do as a consultant – an objective view is sometimes necessary if people are getting too close to what will be done, so pick a colleague with no reason to flatter you).

All this means there is certainly oppportunity to extend learning and practice, and, make no mistake, whatever you may have done already, presentational skill cannot have too much practice, providing, that is, you remain objective and are prepared to analyse honestly what you do (and take on board any feedback from others). Then you can ensure your techniques improve continually. Within an organization it may help to improve skills if people are:

- encouraged to rehearse what they have to do
- encouraged also to seek out additional opportunities to increase practice opportunities (some companies run internal talks, make certain internal meetings more formal than might otherwise be necessary, and take other similar actions to provide such occasions).

Depending on your position this may be a process you can play a part with, encouraging members of your staff if you are a manager, for instance.

The rewards in corporate and career terms of developing good presentational skills are considerable. What is more, good habits do set in, a process that is more likely if you set out to make it so. If you develop the habit of preparing, for example, and develop good habits regarding exactly how you go about it, then you will find your whole approach will act to help the end result. A good structure for notes will prompt you to ask yourself if there should be a visual aid at certain points and whether there are sufficient of them overall, and to do this more certainly and effectively. Good and sufficient visual aids will, in turn, augment the presentation.

The thinking and the process create a positive loop. Moreover, practice will soon begin to take some of the chore out of the whole process. Preparation does not take so long for those who know how to go about it and have a good system for doing so, for example. Even awkward factors, such as judging how long a message will take to run through, become more certain with practice.

Beyond all this, to a degree, the sky is the limit. The best presenters make it look very easy, though this may simply disguise careful preparation, rehearsal and execution. Training, study and simply practice and sensible consideration of how you have done can help everyone move towards an acceptable standard. But it can do more than this. Charisma, often regarded (indeed defined) as a gift, actually consists (certainly in part) of intentionally applied techniques. Good eye contact, appropriate verbal emphasis, a careful choice of words and gestures, the confidence to hold a pause – and more – all cumulatively add to the charisma rating someone may be regarded as projecting. But they can all be learned, developed and deployed to enhance the overall effect. This is not to say that the process is contrived. Something like a genuine enthusiasm is infectious. For the rest, in many ways it adds up to a respect for the audience and the occasion. The last thing people want is to sit through a lack-lustre presentation. Those who work at it, use the techniques and let their personality contribute, make the best job of it, helping both the audience and themselves. The alternative, a dreary presentation and an audience who resent it, is not a happy one.

Thank you for reading this far. I hope the content of this book will have acted as a catalyst, giving you some ideas both to implement and deploy immediately and others to work on and adapt. The rest is up to you. You are the only coach who is always there when you make a presentation. If you have already had some practice, considering what you are doing against the knowledge of the principles set out here will help you seek an even higher standard. If you are nervously awaiting your first outing: go for it. You now know something of the techniques involved and how they can assist. Aim to surprise yourself; and your audience.'

Sits down. Sighs with relief. Imagines filing the notes under 'Never again', and contemplates a large drink.

When audiences come to see us authors lecture, it is largely in the hope that we'll be funnier to look at than to read
Sinclair Lewis

Further Information

Training in presentations skills

For readers who are in management or supervisory positions within an organization or group perhaps I might add a final suggestion. If you would like to develop the presentation skills of others or use this book as part of a training programme in presentation skills you will find my training manual *Ready Made Activities for Presentations Skills* a useful resource. This sets out how to conduct an internal workshop to develop the skills of a group, and is designed for the manager as much the trainer. As such it offers a complete guide to exactly how to proceed, and is designed to minimize preparation and ensure the session works well. It draws on the same core material as this one and is published by Pitman Publishing. It is available, as they say, from all good bookshops.

Patrick Forsyth

Appendix

How are you doing?

As was said in the Afterword, you are your own best tutor. However, it is difficult to simply say to yourself: 'How did that go?' – there are, as we have seen, too many things going on. We end therefore with a checklist (figure 13 on the following page) to help you assess your current standard, your progress or that of colleagues (it can be used on your own or in consultation).

The checklist contains many of the key elements to keep in mind, under four overall headings: *Content*, *Structure*, *Manner* and *Maintenance of Interest*. There are some spaces at the end to enter additional headings if you wish. Next to the headings there is a column for your 'score'. Here you can give yourself or your colleague marks from one to four for performance. This will show you the areas you need to work on. The key is to maintain an endless vigil and always search for ways of improving.

Figure 13. *Presentation performance checklist*

Content – what was said	score	Structure – arrangement of content	score	Manner – and the impression it made	score	Maintenance of interest – appeal to audience	score
Understandable		Clear objective		Physical appearance		Focus on audience	
Well-selected		Overall direction		Stance		Enthusiasm	
Level of detail		Signposting		Gestures		Examples	
Level of technicality		*Beginning*: • effective start • statement of intent		Presence		Illustration	
Logical sequence		*Middle*: • logical progression		Projection		Humour	
Power of description		*End*: • summary • action request • highnote		Rapport		*Aids*: • appropriate method • clear • match what is said • illustrative	
Evidence		Continuity		Empathy			
Link to documentation		Focus on key points		Pace		Audience involvement	
Relevance to audience		Timing		Eye contact		'Flourish'	
				Voice (variety & emphasis)		Animation	
				Management (of aids/ environment)			
				Sensitivity (to difficult issues)			

Index

accidents 78
agreement 55
alcohol 58
appearance 14
arms 75
articulation 69
audibility 64
audience 7, 14, 46, 101

beginning 48
behaviour 60
butterflies 19

career skills 1
cartoon 91
chairmanship 109
characteristics of presenter 4
clarity 52
communications 13
confidence 18

deciding content 31
description 54
difficulties 13
dry mouth 19

emphasis 63, 65, 72
ending 56
enthusiasm 50
environment 22
equipment check 99
exhibits 98

eye contact 20, 60

fear *see* nerves
feedback 56
flip chart 92
flourishes 83
footwork 74
fragility 3

gaining attention 48
gestures 77
gobbledegook 69

handouts 95
hands 19, 75
hearing 14
humour 85

inflection 67
interruptions 78, 80

language 53

manner 60
microphone 99
middle 31
mindmapping 31
misunderstanding 13

nerves 9, 16
number (in audience) 20

objections 106

objectives 29
overhead projector (OHP) 89, 97

pace 65
perception 12
performance appraisal 117
pitch 69
preparation 17, 28
punctuation 71
purpose 2
putting over the content 52

questions 101

rapport 50
reading 28
reasons (for presentation) 7
recording 64, 66
rehearsal 37
review 37

self talk 42
sequence 52

setting objectives 29
signposting 45
slides 18, 89
social events 8
sounds 69
speaker's notes 35, 37
stance 74
structure 48
summary 57

table top presenter 94
team presentation 41
thanks 58
timing 15, 56, 82
training 5

unexpected accidents 78
unforeseen incidents 80

visual aids 54, 89
voice 25, 55, 63

whiteboard 95
word choice 66